B. GREEN'S DESCRIPTIVE POETRY & PROSE

1940 -2021

The painting on the cover is by IVY LANDWEHR.
The date is unknown.
Poem by B. Green 16/2/2018.

The Poetry is of Confessional and
Autobiographical style

Published by Bernard A. N. Green

ISBN 978-0-9576042-3-0

13/12/2021

Printed by Biddles Books, King's Lynn,
Norfolk, PE32 1SF

Contents

THERE IS A PLEASURE IN BEING MAD WHICH NONE BUT THE MAD MAN KNOW

Reference an Irish Fancy 1822.

I must be mad, for writing so many assorted poems and stories in my books.

But it has given me a tremendous amount of pleasure from the reaction of people.

There are nine different types of poems in this book,
Poems for ladies, men, and the young. Predictive poems,
Poems about nature. Poems about Politicians. War and
Immigration.

Then there are Haiku and Senryu.

The Haiku is about nature.
The Senryu is about human foibles.
They consist of 3-phrases of 5-7-5 syllables.
and are a Japanese style of poem.

I wish to thank Mr Nigel Mitchell of Biddles Books for his tremendous amount of help that he gave me during the writing of my variety of books.

MY WORD

I found poetry when I found word
It corrects the spelling of every word
Being dyslexic was to me; a bind
WORD gave me; peace of mind
Writing gives me relaxation
and an inner satisfaction
I became literate, changed my world
I now communicate around the world

SNOWFLAKES EQUALS EARTHQUAKES

Snow what miracles you do perform
but you do not take the world by storm
These tasks are done by gentle persuasion
Take care, it is not soft on every occasion

Snow lands with a touch so light
often in the dark, long winter night
We awake to something we cannot understand
we fear, look and listen, it is quiet across the land

We have become used to constant sound
aircraft above, cars, lorries, rumble across the ground
When suddenly there is no noise, reaching our ears
it takes a little time to equate, to quell our fears

Continued

Then when the child and the child in me
see the white expanse, 'Snow' we shout with glee
When young, have you rolled naked in the snow?
then quickly ran into the house with healthy glow

Now when older, when blood runs slow
desist, resist, just let the youngsters go
Wild animals and birds, do not have the same delight
it can cause starvation, finding food, a constant fight

Softly, softly, gently touching, building deep
at first the fluffy feel, easy to move, to sweep
As ice it forms into exciting sharp prisms
it freezes into solid piles, creating prisons

What is not seen is the weight it can create
it crushes roofs to devastate, avalanches suffocate
The first signs of the weight it has, mass
electric cables snap, trees come down, crash

The world of ice and snow, the Polar Poles
have reason to be there, they have roles
Their part is to control the weather
and the ocean currents, now that is clever

The Earth is a balloon with a heavy ice crown
The ice, miles thick, is pressing down
Allow the ice to disappear, to melt
and the balloon will adjust, it will be felt

Continued

The Pole area will rise up, move and lift
This action will cause Tectonic plates to shift
that is why we now have so many earthquakes
Global warming, man's ineptitude is what it takes.

Note. I wrote the poem called Snowflakes Equals Earthquakes on 21/1/2010 and was surprised to find that on 2/7/2010 a science program on TV stated that Glacier's ice melting increases volcanic activity. I believe its technical name is Post-glacial rebound.
Also on TV the 28/05/15 Secrets of the Earth seismologists said that large reservoirs cause stress on faults by the waters mass depressing the earth's crust (North West Research). But this effect is nothing compared to the relief of pressure by the melting of the glaciers and polar ice-cap with global warming, which will result in the earth's crust re-adjusting its equilibrium.

This coupled with the rising sea levels which will also alter the earth's delicate balancing act. Expect Earthquakes.
You will have seen on the news, the devastation in Tonga by the earthquake in the South Pacific Ocean on Sat 15/01/2022.
Expect more of these!

THE POPULATION EXPLOSION

Fragile Earth has a thin veneer, not all of it is habitable
Only part of its land mass is productive and liveable
that can provide safe shelter, food and water
All species eventually outgrow their space
and that applies to the human race
Politics call for greater growth
It's too late for our species
living in rubbish, faeces
Far too many people
It's unsustainable
and unstoppable
Armageddon
is soon
Boom
FIN

Note. In 1946 at school a chart was shown to my class predicting the growth pattern for the world population. It looked like what we now know looks like an atomic mushroom cloud. I was then 12 years old. The sustainable level of human occupation is about 2 billion. There are now about 7billion. An Asteroid crashing into earth is required to change all that. A natural pandemic or perhaps it will be a chemical or biological war that will decimate the population.

This poem was published in my book Dunce or Dyslexic on the 13th December 2012.

1945-49

My teachers hit me
Had not heard of Dyslexia
WORD helps me create

Haiku 5-7-5 syllables. WORD is on Microsoft

SHIPS Senryu

Build ships higher still
They turn over much easier
Income is higher

Note. There is approx. thirty feet below water and hundreds of feet above! If you jumped from the top decks of these modern ships you would most probably break your bones.

Modern ships have stabilizer fins which tempt the
shipping companies to build them higher and higher.
What happens when they stop working?
The ship will be unstable. This can happen with a loss of electricity.

TWO THOUGHTS

Seeds, thoughts
Plant or write
Bring great rewards.

Overpopulation
Brings pandemics
Renews the balance.

AUTUMNAL THOUGHTS

When I was five, Mother dragged me crying, to school
Teachers had not heard of dyslexic, I was called a fool
After entering the Victorian buildings hall
I saw four posters on the schoolroom wall

Transfixed by the varied colours across the board
I stared at the Autumn scene, that I just adored
In beautiful chromolithograph colours
I forgot all about, those three others

Seventy years on, I still enjoy Autumn colour
My love of life, and life in England is no duller
The myriad shades of green and yellow, spots of red
interspersed with brown, of trees now dead

Shafts of sunlight, through the trees does filter
shining on the Birch trees with their subtle silver
Golden leaves showering down upon your head
fallen leaves, a mulch to put the seeds to bed

Continued

Teacher gave me a Sand-Box to write in then
That was 1939, I had already used a fountain pen
I only learnt to type when aged seventy-four
enabling me to overcome difficulties I'd met before

It is computer spellcheck that enables me
to write and tell you, what I feel and see
I am not a poet to be remembered in perpetuity
Just writing, fills me with fun and sense of glee

Note. Sand-Box was a shallow tray, with a layer of sand. The pupil wrote in the sand with their finger a letter or figure then shook the tray to level the sand for the next letter or word.

ZEITGEIBER

Even the blind appreciate daylight
Warmth compensating the cold of night

We are all entrained to the circadian rhythm
It tells plants when to grow and flower, ahem

BERNARD ALFRED NORMAN GREEN.
MARCHING TO HIS FUTURE AT
ALDERSHOT LIDO IN HAMPSHIRE 1938

TIME DISTANCE DESIRE

Mother pushed me in a pram to her door
She took short steps when I was four
My turn to go, to walk, a long way, then
I am a big boy, now about the age of ten

It is a very long way, many miles I'm sure
Now I know, it is only just past the store
Tall chimney belching thick black smoke
Cooking children or burning coal or coke?

The house looked damp, dingy dark and old
Stone walls looked wet, covered with mould
In a clearing, the spinney, the sun rarely sees
Short of the beneficial rays, bad for the bees

Set among the natural growth, disorder
not in modern regular squares and border
I wander down the beaten path. A lawn
how is it kept so neatly cut and shorn?

Sandy soil, no human gardeners are here
Pine trees, Birch, Holly and Oak, Roe Deer
Each day furry gardeners chew and nibble
leaving patches of heather in the middle

This house, which I thought was a witches den
gave ambition for such a garden, a heartfelt yen
It took me thirty years, at age forty, I got it then
Ferns, heather, trees. Deer nibbled grass, its heaven.

Note. This is the same house as in the Village Witch poem.

TRODDEN SNOW

Our life is like treading on virgin snow
Be careful how you tread it
for every mark you leave, will show

Note. I like the sentiment behind these few words. This was quoted to my wife in Malaysia in 1961. The origin is unknown.

LOOK AT THE MOTHER BROTHER

When you start to think of marriage
I expect you'd like to go in a carriage
Not use a forklift and low loader lorry
or phone the fire service for the soiree

If you like your women large and fat
there are plenty of them, so that's that
But if you want a woman that is lean
there are not many, from what I have seen

You see, it is not a case of having bad genes
It's French fries, Soda, cakes and custard creams
lack of willpower, over-indulgence of a child
creates flab, fatness not found in the wild

So, when you look at your girlfriend's mother
and don't enjoy the sight. Don't bother, brother.

CATHEDRAL OF TREES

Just a country road in Surrey
Which makes me want to slow
and enjoy the peace and quiet
Away from the hustle and bustle
the wind makes the leaves rustle
A cathedral of trees reach high above
The changing colours of the leaves
can compete with leaded windows
There is a sermon from a collard dove above
then birds start twittering the hymn
A delight to be away from traffic din

SCHOOL IN 1946

The teacher sharpened his pencil
I admired his dexterity, his style
Now I know it was displacement activity

He used a small silver penknife
Staccato movements of his flicking hand
It was show time, a display, an Art Form

The girls got cuddles, and extra tuition
Boys got short thrift, and punched on the head
His fist had three gold rings, one like twisted rope

I'm dyslexic I got hit a lot, Roy Jarvis got hit very hard
It started his epileptic fits, caused revengeful thoughts
Thwarted, fortunately he died early, heart attack.

Note. This was East Street School, Farnham Surrey, UK 1946.

LOONY MOONY

I love not the moon
To some a magic notion
Its steady path
but a mechanical motion
I prefer the stormy sea
The volcanic eruption
which reminds me
of attraction and seduction

COCCOON

It is better to live dangerously
A short life lived to the full
than have a dull existence.

SWEET AND SOUR

Mother told me
girls are nice
They are made of
sugar and spice

Boys are always fighting
They are very bad
Play football, get dirty
Get sweaty, like your Dad

Girls are cuddly, soft
They look pretty in pink
Like dolls and furry things
Boys don't wash, like to stink

Girls, if they listen to mother
learn to play sweet, soft & shy
To convince men of their need
for expensive things to buy

Continued

I asked, Mum can I have a dress
I was not at all, soft and shy
Wanted to be a girl to miss the war
Looked so cute, in pink. Oh my!

Then I learnt about child birth
I had thought women had it made
A bitter-sweet pill to swallow for me
It made my jealousy of girls fade.

Note. I was probably about ten years of age and knew that men had to go to war. Women stayed at home, and it seemed that they had a better deal in life. My mother dressed me up one day and took a photograph of me, after a few hours I hated it and decided to be all male.

PALESTINE Haiku. Year 2021

Israel bombs farms
Starving Palestinians
Weapon of war

DESPERATE JOURNEY Senryu

Ethiopia drought
Economic immigrants
Will increase yearly

TO VALUE A MAN

To value a man, to find his worth or infamy
Number his friends, more than five, too many
A successful man is often quite a louse
conversely with no enemies, a mouse
Remember where your family live and breathe
friends! When you are in trouble they leave
Don't try and die a multi-millionaire
just do your best in everything and care
If this is done and you try your best
fate will always take care of the rest

RELEASE, RELIEF, RENEWAL

You can release that inner turmoil
We all miss that turning, hit the rut
get on the wrong road
Write, un-tie that knot in your gut

When a person writes, and creates
a story, poem, prose or ode
It will show a state of mind
a mood, modus vivendi, mode

We are all subject to moody moods
fits of madness or despair
Doubts, regrets, remorse are with us all
writing helps to sooth and clear the air.

18/02/2010

YOUTH

Oh, brash youth
I envy your ignorance
Unaware of serious pain

BUCKET BOY

We lived in a house in nineteen forty-three
No electric light, inside toilet, bath or TV
Daddy, Mummy, Midge, Nita, Storm, Gale and me
I was called Bucket boy, why? You will see

We had an outdoor toilet called a Bog, or Loo
at night we used a bucket, to pee, No poo!
My elder sister with wicked grin, and look of glee
would fill the bucket over the very top with wee

So much so, it was above the edge, the lip
I had to carry it down the stairs, dare not trip
How could that be, so high? Her action's so low.
Above the bucket edge? Surface tension, now I know

Bath time was not much fun, you will laugh.
Seven of us, in one five foot long, tin bath
Boiling water from a kettle, you jumped out fast
when deeper dirtier, hotter, dad was always last

Continued

Not all at once, shallow water, baby first, out quick
Tilley lamps to pump, Paraffin lamps, trim the wick
Candles light the way to bed, upstairs, no coal fire
un-heated bedrooms, cold starched sheets, dire

My bedroom wall was lined with Hop Bag sacking
Mum had glued wallpaper with flour, mice kept snacking
We even had a TV Ariel on the roof, it was false, a fake
we did not have a set. It was for the neighbour's sake

I had a healthy, reasonably happy childhood
Mum was an angel, and dad like Robin Hood
Mum didn't understand and paddled my bum
I was dyslexic and a slow learner not dumb.

MIGRANTS Senryu

Migrants at border
Now building barbed fence
Soon they might lay mines

HOP PICKING

Spring is here and very green
Hop vines are climbing
seeking the warming sun

Harvesting of hops, long gone
I miss the smell of hops
freshly picked by nimble fingers

Raw sore fingertips
from those rough vines that
hops use to climb the strings

The strings tied in the spring
by men walking on stilts
between the lines of poles

Poles ten feet high running
across the landscape
until they meet the sky

The pickers locals, gypsies
women, old men and children
crowded into the lanes

Workers pulled down the vines
women and old men picking
talking singing, children playing

Continued

Huge wicker baskets hold the hops
A big basket contained a bushel
the measure by which the farmer paid

He looked for tricks, leaves and sticks
Tricks of the pickers to cheat and
bulk up their bushel baskets

It did not succeed
to bulk up their pay
at the end of the day

The baskets were placed on a cart
drawn by two huge shire horses
to the old mill, to be dried

Then pressed into a hessian bale
at least eight feet long
this system is now long gone

A world for which I long
But would not like to return
for those days we were really poor

THEY SAW WARSAW Haiku

Israel knows of Siege
They saw the Siege of Warsaw
Starvation and Death

Note. Warsaw Oct 1939-May 1943.

BED

The idea of bed has changed for me
when I became seventy -three
I no longer thought of or pondered
about extending the family tree

FAME AND SHAME

When a celebrity gets a name
in their quest for fame
Social drinking is the start
then so-called soft drugs take part

Doctors and agents encourage their use
and the star then sinks into drug abuse
It is akin to riding on a runaway train
when constant rehearsing is a strain

Taking pills to sleep or keep awake
to promote energy, other drugs they take!
Then they start to slide into deep decline
until they hit the end of the line.

It seems that once in the limelight
celeb's cannot quietly slide out of sight

TOILET, TO LET FOR A PENNY

Whilst sitting, you have time to reflect
on the methane you produce, and effect
When you are in this daily act
please read my study on the fact
that you are creating methane
which for the environment is a bane.

As you spend a penny or number two
I will now attempt to relieve you
of any down in the dumps feeling of guilt
by showing the process is lined with gilt
So don't be in too much haste
to dispose of this useful waste.

You can be an important player
in protecting the ozone layer
Mixed together with this and that
and enzymes, hit with electricity in a vat
This process will create hydrogen gasses
to run cars and transport for the masses.

Washing with water, reducing use of toilet roll
to help protect the ozone layer is our goal
Also save the trees to stop erosion of soil
And reduce dependence on expensive oil
If unfortunately you tend to blow off, fart
don't spray tinned chemicals, please play your part

Note. A pennyworth of thoughts, on spending a penny. Soon you will have to spend a Pound, Euro or a Dollar.

SHENGAN AGREEMENT

If I went to Africa without money
but with my Human Rights
How far would I get? Nowhere
unlike England, land of milk and honey

REGENERATE OR DEPOPULATE

The World renews itself, regenerates
Volcanic action builds Mountains
sinks Islands, builds Islands
by the action of tectonic plates

Earth can only support so much life
Man and woman are smothering,
covering Mother Earth's productive land
this will bring starvation and strife

Palm Oil plantations in straight lines drive
across the small farms valley's and hills
that was renewable healthy countryside
Now only rats and snakes will survive

As the Polar ice completes its thaw
We are told twenty kilometers
of land will be under the sea, then
hundred million displaced people or more

Continued

The World was once clean, now I despair
what I see around me is now in decline
It's not renewable; it's in a state of disrepair
water shortages, rising sea, very bad air

A perpetual time machine, you think
It is not, the dish will quickly fill
All space taken countries annexed
spoils of war, it happens in an eyelid blink

We live in a world full of lies and hype
International ventures,space travel
Be careful of our leaders, they say
we must prevail, you know the type

How many cows can inhabit a field?
without fecal contamination
There is a limit, old farmers knew
Everyone must consider the safe yield

How many sheep can graze?
on an acre without spoiling
the ground, the old one's knew
They knew the limit in the old days

How many goats does it take?
to eat everything in sight
Even the roots of next year's grass
they leave only desert in their wake

More land will not be heaven sent
The desert will extend its dry
unproductive sandy wastes
Are you preparing for this event?

Continued

Humans take land to produce meat
using precious limited resources
which could grow fruit and vegetables
How much goes for cats and dogs to eat

Victorians used dog poo to soften leather
it produced the softest white gloves
Now dog walkers put poo in plastic bags
and throw it in bushes where it stays forever.

Note. Be careful of those political leaders that have led sheltered lives and those people born in so called High Ivory Towers. They do not know the hardships that the so called common people endure. I think more people with an agricultural background should be involved in political reform, not statisticians.

Written 2015

THE VILLAGE WITCH

The little lad looked at the house
It was me, a humble little mouse
I had heard someone say, "She is a witch,"
Or perhaps they said. "She is a bitch,"

There was a dank smell, like cloth burning
smouldering, smelly, stomach churning
With a wish, I threw a penny in her well
Is she a witch? No sound, it never fell

Tall towering trees, hanging over
No rabbits run, there is no clover
Timid tapping on the tremendous door
Opening abruptly, I fell down on the floor

Tock-tick, Tock-tick, the clock was Tocking?
Day, date dial, face quietly looking, mocking
The clock was angry with me, I could tell
It said Click clack, stared, and rang its bell

Stressing its size and importance Tack-Tock
Repeating itself Tack-Tock, I am a big clock
Gloom and doom, the old lady sits in the damp
Fluttering, guttering light from paraffin lamp

Sitting, sniffing, sewing away her final years
Lonely, bony, gaunt face but not crying tears
Will this witch throw me into her well?
Her bright blue eyes held me in her spell

continued

Tea-time is here, would you like some cake
she cackled, the scrumptious scones I did bake
She did me proud, fed me well, very nice tea
Was she trying to fatten me, then to eat me?

But that lady was good to me and kind
Sadly, I cannot picture her face in my mind
She opened the huge door, to a fairy dell
seen now, it is small, was I under her spell

She showed me round her secret garden glade
Heather, foxgloves, ferns, natural not man-made
Our conversation of that day has gone
But memories of that garden have shone

It has stayed with me, those quiet floral glades
Bright sunlight on leaves and soft sunlit shades
The wind wafted down golden pollen showers
foxgloves fluttered their bell-shaped flowers

Walking me to the gate she said, "thank you, goodbye,"
Chaffinches chattered in her hedge as I passed them by
Now my own garden is like hers, a Fairy glade
It has taken me over forty years to get it made

Proof that events as a child are deeply implanted
and in later years you can have those wishes granted

Notes. This house is in the road into Sands Village, near Farnham. It is now named Burnt Stocks. I wonder if originally it was called Burnt Socks from little children that the wicked Witch cooked?

Stocks. This is the name of a type of brick.

THE TELEGRAM

Devised to pass information quickly
to out-perform pigeon and pony express
The telephone was too informal
Questions could be asked, more distress

Letters were too slow for business
not many people had a telephone
Business used them to inform the recipient
before the newspapers hit the home

There was joy in the message of a birth
and pleasure to get a wedding invitation
Fear of receiving the OHMS telegram
and then the opening of it, in trepidation

With his pillbox hat, blood red jacket
Jaunty, happy delivery man said
Telegram Ma'am. It read, John Doe,
your son injured in action. Now dead

Note. Telegrams were used in those days, it made me think of the awful moment during the war when families received these short sharp, to the point messages.

SNOW

Children love to frolic in the snow
The adults say nice and pretty
but want it to quickly go
the dangers of a crash are there
If you have to drive to work, so
children's pleasure, you cannot share

As the snow blankets the countryside
giving a sense of peace and quiet, but belies
the struggle to survive, hibernate or hide
Deep snow around our house, we were stuck
for ten days in two thousand and nine, very
bitter, but it turned out to be a bit of luck

Writing stories and poetry I did try
then happened by happy chance
to find a web site to write my poetry
Response from poets was encouraging
I enjoy the challenge, the repartee
and it keeps the brain cells working

I retired years ago, and have tried
to relive those childish moments
on a hill, which I have, to slide
But soon the cold caused fingers to numb
I retreat indoors to my country seat where
I sit by the fire to nurse and warm my bum.

Note. Sliding down a hill on a plastic bag is fast and fun that is until you hit a tree stump, with your bum.

JOY

The joy of smoking
five members of family
they are all deceased.

Haiku. Poor them, poor you if you smoke.

TELLING THE TRUTH

"Son that was a fib you told
Do not tell porky-pies, for telling
lies, I'll smack you, for fibs, a scold."
Later a policeman visited my dad
and talked about this and that
A quiet chat, is what they had

After he had gone, I ask, why?
I heard you lie to that nice man
"Be quiet, or I will make you cry;"
But you told me, never to lie
"Ah, you see there is a difference
sometimes you have to, to get by"

Some people get upset, when you tell the truth
so then a little fib called a white lie
helps to calm, stops them being uncouth
Sometimes when seeing trouble loom
a white lie can sometimes help
to assist, to pacify, or to groom

Continued

It enables you to elaborate, so to speak
And sometimes using a white lie
avoids hurt feelings, or appearing weak
Perhaps it is best, to alter truth, to lie
to your husband, wife or child to calm
and soothe. That is a called a porky-pie

To be totally truthful, is I think impossible
Would you tell the police, you were speeding?
or passed a red light. You would be in trouble
If you did a first Bungee jump or Sky-dive
and said you were not frightened
you were lying, because fear keeps you alive.

A MORON Senryu

Only a male moron
would pay to shoot a black rhino
to feel a Big Man

TWO RE-OCCURING DREAMS

In a clearing, lying naked in the sun
behind Holmfields away from everyone
When a neighbor's wife, walked close by
"Hallo Bernard", she said "Hallo." Said I
She passed without a falter in her step or style
no glimmer of a grin, or sliver of a smile
Well, she had a teenager son
and was a woman with a sense of fun

The second dream, a memory of a nightmare
is always frightening, remembering I was there
I and friends set out to climb over a cave with gates
I was small of build then, and mixing with big mates
Getting above the cave quickly, they helped me.
Above Mother Ludlum's cave was a sandy scree
I was slipping, sliding towards a drop. I freeze
fearing to fall fifteen feet, friends laughing and tease
Eventually realizing the danger, form a chain
and free me, I could never ever climb again.

Notes Mother Ludlam's Cave is by the river Wey and quite close to Waverley Abbey ruins. It was a famous watering hole for Victorians. Mrs Ludlam did live in the cave in the 1800's but was accused of being a witch and was chased away. I believe that her largest cooking pot is kept in the church at Frensham.

Holmfields was a large Victorian house in Runfold near Farnham, Surrey that had with 23 rooms that my father purchased for £3,000 after WW2. I had been occupied by Canadian soldiers and towards the end of the war German and Italian prisoners, many Italians settled in this area after the war mainly by starting work on the farms.

TUTANKHAMUN

Tutankhamun was ruler of men
This was quite a manly task
Why was he buried in a woman's mask?
His death was unexpected and no
funeral arrangements were made
So they used second hand items.
The mask was made for a woman
so they modified it, with a beard.

THE BLACK WATCH

Soldiers had been in requisitioned Victorian houses throughout the war in our village called Runfold. Twenty roomed mansions on big estates, they were playgrounds for my-self and my friend Roy, the year was 1944. These properties had gardens full of exotic plants and trees. The house ceilings were twelve feet high and full of ornament, plaster patterns, rooms were huge, twenty by thirty feet wide. It did feel like heaven, it nearly was.

I admired Black Watch Badges, on their beret
We collected Army stuff, most given, some found!
Badges were hard to obtain, Roy wanted a bayonet
Thinking the Scottish troops were all on parade
we walked through the imposing mahogany doors
up curving stairs with carved rampant lions, handmade

Continued

A room eight beds, kit laid out with the kilts and finery.
Sash windows wide open, a warm English summer day.
There a badge, for plucking, bayonet for Roy's armoury.
I am in the middle of the room, this the second floor
A red headed, kilted apparition appeared, bayonet fixed.
Roy, hidden from this monsters sight, behind the bedroom door.

With bayonet pointed at me, he charged, screaming a curse.
Full of fright and too small to fight, I turned to flight, I
dived head-first out the open window. Now roles in reverse.
Landing on my back in a dense bush, I lay taking stock.
A fall of about eighteen feet, accounting for front doorsteps.
A good job I did not land on an iron fence or a rock

The sergeant appeared at the window, in a state of shock.
He never spoke; I rolled off that bushy bush and ran away
Next day there was a gentle knock on our house door,
When mother opened the door that bright sunny day
I saw him framed by rays of sunlight through the door
Mother told me "Go away." He spoke to her in a funny way

Demobilization for the troops. 1945, end of strife
I suppose it was my fault she went off with that Scot
Five hundred miles away to Auchtermuchty in Fife.
She came back, years later to stay with my dad
I enjoyed having a mum, a few more years
She eventually left, after three more kids were had

Continued

In 1972, I bought Alfs Café Runfold from my father
My mother had remarried, my father soon died
I did not serve very often; dyslexia puts me in a lather
It was 1994 40yrs gone by, then on a bright summer day
I was serving; it was a busy day in the café on the A31
In the doorway he stood, I knew it was him straight away

"You don't know me," he started to say, looking harried
"I do, you're the Scot from Auchtermuchty," I said.
"Is your mother still around?" "Yes, in Farnham, remarried,"
I said, "Wait a minute," as he stepped back, he disappeared
I wanted to talk. My mother would have loved to see him
Within a precious minute, he had gone. That was weird.

Notes. I ran out looking for him, but he had gone so quickly.
My mother was very upset to find she had missed the opportunity to see him, we never heard or saw him again. I never learnt his surname.
Mother said life in a Scottish croft was too hard and remote.
Was the visit by his ghost?

The Victorian mansion was opposite Alf's Café in Runfold and was called Larchfield. After the soldiers left it was a hostel occupied by The Land Army girls. After they disbanded, the house was demolished and a Sandpit Company called Ebenezer Mears extracted the sand below. The foreman named Lou Westbrook lived in the house next to the café. The pit was eventually filled with rubbish.

THE NEW TIBET

Zimbabwe has accepted the Chinese Yuan
as its currency. Do not ignore this or yawn

Now its farmers must pay a land tax
China will rule as Zimbabwean's relax

Note. The countries present leaders will gradually lose their role as the Chinese money men assume all control through the operation of railways and construction.

SEE YOU LATER

I'm a waiter on the P.O ship 'Chusan'
London to Australia via Hong Kong
Assigned to my table three men, a woman
She, mixed French,Chinese full of Joie de vivre,
Named Mac, she had a Scottish ancestor
Vivacious, brunette, and very talkative
Three weeks pass, in the Indian Ocean
She said something to me, which, when said now
creates memories, amusement, and emotion

continued

I took it as a directive, I'm eighteen, she twenty-four
rising from the table, she whispered, "See you later,"
I'd never heard this before, now I know its Au Revoir.
Rushing to my quarters, shower brush teeth and hair
Pretend to be on duty, I put perfume on here and there
Entered the dining room. Damn, there's the purser
Droppped down on to the floor, crawling under the tables
where this morning I scrubbed. Anything to pursue her,
walk, head held high, pretend a service to perform, I had!
I'm there, tap, tap, door opens. A half-clad vision appears
"Hallo, what can I do for you." she asked, I must be mad!

"You said, see you later," I announced. I'm worried, fraught.
She said, "I am sorry, but I did not mean it that way."
I cannot go back yet, it's too early, I will be caught
The cabin was hot, here in the Indian Ocean
"Ok, stay a while, I have letters to type, sit down
She typed very fast, fingers in a blur of motion
Salacious thoughts rose to mind then dims and dies
I sit silently, salivating at the sight, then she throws
a pillow at me and said, "Please cover those eyes."

She removed the pillow after what seemed an eternity
and stood there almost naked, a perfect female form.
Firm breasts, nipples showing though her negligee
Next day, telegraphed my dad. Send savings do not tarry
He ignored my demand for he had spent all of it.
This was like a dream, it wasn't, I wished to marry
Then I found she was to disembark in Singapore
It was difficult to act as her waiter, to be remote
She was to marry an officer in an English Army Corps

continued

In Singapore, she left to meet her fiancée, her hunk
I went ashore to drink, walking back there she was
He in uniform, Sam Brown belt with pistol gun, I'm drunk
I run towards a roundabout that I thought was grass
Athletic as a drunk can be, I did a somersault
to lay there till they passed, landed on my arse
It was solid; it was tarmac, in the evening light
I mistook it for soft grass, a bed on which to lay
to sleep off my sorrow, in pain I scream in fright

Above me appeared a kindly face, a gentleman
"Are you alright," he asked of me that night
I reply, "Yes thanks, I know you are Mac's man"
Then passing out, I slept. Next day aboard the ship
apparently in anger, with pistol in hand he chased
her round the ship, untill she gave him the slip
In a first-class cabin she stowed away
to flee down the Straits of Malacca
and ended up in Hong Kong WMCA

Then she sailed on a Greek ship to Australia
before I returned from Sydney three weeks later
I do hope, life has been good and kind to her.
Take care of what you say.
Be careful what you think you hear,
it might haunt you another day.

Notes. The Merchant Navy

My first ship was the P&O STRATHNAVER No 162619, taking cargo and passengers to Australia via the Suez Canal. My wage as a Bell Boy was £9 per month. I was discharged from the Merchant Navy on the 2/10/1953 with my last month's pay being £24. This ship weighed 22,500 tons and could carry 573 1st class passengers and 496 Second Class. There was no air conditioning, compare that with the huge

cruise ships of today. I joined the P&O ship CHUSAN No 183248 on 12/7/1952. This ship was the first to fit Denny-Brown stabilizers to stop seasickness. A three-week cruise around the Mediterranean Sea cost £106 in First Class and £61 in Second Class.
The Second-class passengers were restricted to the stern or rear of the ship and had separate dining rooms with plate service, whereas the First Class had full silver service and a much better menu.

CANNOT COMPUTE

Young people are becoming too dependent
on computers and losing social skills
What will happen when the system goes dead?
Have you noticed at shop checkout till's
youngsters cannot calculate in their head.

THINK ABOUT STINK

Beware the air freshener spray
That purports to brighten your day
It kills the smell by clogging the cells
In your nose, that detect those smells

Can it aggravate your lungs or is it mild
does it affect the breathing of a child?
Propane propellant projects the perfume
Light your match and it will go boom.

The can states, 'Do not inhale the spray' Why?
Put a light to it and you will see why!

MY PASSION

I moulded her to my desire,
Shaped her by devious means
Pulled and puffed her lips
Tucked in the tiny waist
I shivered looking at that
Shapely curvaceous shape
Her colour, a light brown
and her bulbous bottom,
She stands scrutiny, good firm body
Undoubtedly, she is my best creation
The best vase you will ever see
Mine from a throw of potter's clay.

ILLUSION, DELUSION (Adult poem)

We walked into the wilderness
Sandy soil, scrub and birch trees
The heather was deep and soft
inviting us to lie down, a soft bed
The darkness closed around us
like a velvet protective cloak

The silence was unusual
as if the darkness muffled all sound
Alone in the darkness, no moon
just the tops of the hills visible
We lay there carefree kissing cuddling
undressing each other carefully, slowly

continued

Warmth of our bodies defied the chill
as we merged into one with each other
I was lost in a crescendo of passion as
she cried out as if in pain as she moved
I knew she was in erotic ecstasy, then
there was a sudden roaring in my ears

It was a military tank moving towards us
but we were in heaven on earth
I not want to move. We will not and we will
become a melange crushed together forever
The engine stopped. We stood up
"I was laid on a wood-ants nest", she said.

Soldiers rose like living dead from fox-holes.
We were in the middle of Army manoeuvres.

23/JUNE/1976.

ACTIVITY

If you can think of something
And visualize it: you can realize it
You can have a dream and think of a scheme
So take rough with smooth

FEEDING FRENZY

I sat in the supermarket, named Tesco
watching the moving human fresco

Delightful damsels with long black hair
from far eastern countries are working there
They have happy faces, seem free of troubles
Their hard-earned cash, sent home, doubles

They send some, some perhaps send all
of their money to mums, in distant Nepal
Perhaps to build a mansion in Kathmandu
If you could do it, you would, wouldn't you

Human Easter Eggs, with short fat legs
totter past, carrying cake and beer in kegs
Old couples, dressed the same way
matching colours, mainly brown and grey

There's mum pushing a heavy overloaded cart
Dad carrying lager and Exchange and Mart
Children crying, I wanted that, I want this
warned, at home you'll get a smack not a kiss

Soldiers in green, heads up, shoulders square
talk loudly, to let you know they are there
Shopping quietly, almost unseen, older men
watch amused, been there, will not again

continued

I sit alone silently watching, drinking coffee
My wife shops, because I'm the man, you see
She likes shopping, she is a real honey
she's spending her own hard-earned money.

It was like watching actors playing their part in a play.
It was like watching actors playing their part in
a moving illustration of a complex chaotic society.

THE FUTURE

We are mortgaging
the future of our children
by our consumption.

EASTER EGGS ON LEGS

Why is it, these days I see on the street
Easter eggs walking on unsteady feet

Is it lack of exercise, I think it is not
it is the mass-produced food we've got

This is the age of instant this and that
a tendency to eat food that makes us fat

Commercial foods are full fats and types of sugar
that means you will never be as fit as a cougar

continued

When young with rationing, Second World War years
you did not see so much weight on their rears

If you need to have surgery, carrying too much weight
Surgeons might have to say. "Sorry you will have to wait"

"You are far too heavy to cope with the anesthetic
Oh, and if you smoke or drink, you can forget it"

Note. This is a problem besetting our society. You have to think about the surgeons also, they do not want overweight patients succumbing under the anesthetic or the knife, and I think it is hard enough to operate on slim people. The hospitals have to think now about compensation pay-outs if things go wrong.

LOST IN A SEA OF EMOTION

I am lost in a sea of personal emotion
Different viewpoints, argument, commotion
like a stormy sea, heaving up and down
Waves in different directions, rain pouring down
cannot decide what decisions to take
No harbour nearby, no radio for a call to make
Run with the wind? Waves will swamp the stern
head into the waves? No spare fuel to burn
Caught between the wind and rough sea
it is like the conflict between she and me
Will the storm pass for winds and waves to fade
if not I'll join Davy Jones, with wrong decisions made

LIFE INSURANCE Senryu

Ads for insurance
Because its profitable
So read the small print

KATHMANDU

Maggie and husband wished to teach in far Nepal
She is English; he spoke with a Canadian drawl
They toured and travelled, arriving in the fall
in the remote region, called Kathmandu
In this part of heaven, quite near Tibet
they taught, and fought (each other) loved
and conceived without hesitation or regret
in the high mountains of Kathmandu

The shop was over twenty miles away
a local hospital not available at all
One could be reached, possibly in one day
in a valley where rivers run in Kathmandu
Maggie was put in a ward with two Nepalese
when the labour pains began to start
Here she felt at home, quite at ease
in the hospital in the wilds of Kathmandu

continued

She went to the bathroom and became aware
that her ward companions' families
were sleeping and cooking in there
In the hospital, in the valley of Kathmandu
In the taps, there was no running water
Then "Caesarean" the visiting surgeon said,
"You are going to have a daughter but
make a' Will', you might die in Kathmandu"

The flies swarmed around for blood
It was like a farce in the hospital theatre
"Keep that fly-swat out of my face, Mahmoud"
the surgeon said during the Op in Kathmandu
A daughter was born, a healthy robust child
Maggie survived, to bear another child, then
the school was blown up by Taliban, it was wild
Her birth certificate says 'Born in Kathmandu'

FRESH AIR

Spray, a bouquet of Fresh Air
In your toilet
Danger; Inflammable Butane.

Note. Kill the smell but be careful not to sniff the spray

THE COLOSSAL COUPLE

Like ancient skin bags full of water
a man a woman son and daughter
Waggling and wobbling with arms out-splayed
they drank tinned Cola as they slowly sashayed

His bulging belly billowing over baggy pants
and sail-like summer shirt to hide all that sags
He with protruding pot belly, perambulating his
pendulous posterior in Pickwickian pantaloons

She with big busts bursting over a bulging belly
sizable sagging bulging bottom bouncing badly
Swaying side to side, arms akimbo they flirt
she swings around in her stupendous saggy skirt

They order large cod, double chips and mushy peas
after every mouthful cover it with salt, if you please
They eat as if it is meant to be a race
cramming ramming food into their face

It is not these peoples fault they are getting obese
What makes you look like a slug. It's not disease
There are preservatives in all mass prepared foods
chemicals that can affect your body and moods

Mind you, is it their fault? I think it is not
as it is people that health education forgot

Note. A day at the Sea-side.

THE GOURMET

Cousin Geoffrey had two heart valves fitted
One was originaly pig and one was knitted
The knitted valve seemed to cause no harm
And it meant he spent less time in the farm
The original valve gives him the snorts and snuffles
So now he spends his time hunting fine truffles.

QUANTITATIVE EASING

A phrase that sounds pleasing. Quantitative Easing
Announcing something that is not so pleasing
No matter how politicians pontificate; claiming validation
and indicate it that it helps you, and stops inflation
Pensioners have seen it all before, it is devaluation
It hurts the poor, devalues the currency of the nation
But if most of your assets are spread abroad
your wealth and future growth is still assured

Note. Politicians and large companies are most likely to have foreign assets and accounts to protect themselves.
It is printing money without assets to back it, like Gold.

POLITICIANS – SCRAP THE LOT

Have you read expense claims by your M.P
The public may ask
If they can do it, why can't we
The lords have their expenses by the thousands
Deprived, the public ask
Can I get cash like that into my calloused hands
When the sick and poor see such things
they should ask the question, why
If I try small petty cheats, heavy penalties it brings
The gold reserves are all but gone, that's been debated
You may ask, why so cheap?
The pension funds have also been badly depleted
Our leaders should by example lead, we'd be led
Perhaps someone had better ask,
Has Parliament's roof been checked? It was covered in lead!

ISRAEL Senryu. Year 2021

They bombed Gaza
Then Israel asked for AID
That's interesting

A WOODLAND WALK

I pondered as I walked the woods
of events in the flora below my knees
We are often blind to nature's wonder
a case of not seeing woods for trees

Think of the grass and the moss
and the myriad of creatures in between
We tread them underfoot without a thought
to us a moss carpet, coloured green

In amongst this, tiny creatures move
between each grassy stalk and stem
To the herbivore and predator alike
each stalk is like a tree to them

Within those stems are creatures
that do not stand and admire the view
They see those stems as we see a forest
and climb each day to drink the dew

Our trees and branches are out of sight
they are part of the great beyond
Perhaps it is their idea of heaven
while balanced on a tiny frond

We live here, their idea of heaven
But should they climb, achieve their aim
they will be eaten by a singing angel
winged and feathered. Bird by name

I am content that I live here
Heaven is not what it seems
We often think of our life as hell
but what awaits, must stay in dreams

ABUSED

Her partner was most brutal
using methods like the Karma Sutra
She now repays all males
by recounting alarming tales
Deeds of terror, many years past
How longer will her pain last?
Her eyes show memories kept, a rack
She should forget, and not look back

AMBER'S OAK

The oak tree had been standing there
for over two hundred years
But now it rots, its branches bare
It is amazing how big you did grow
and from your hillside vantage point
you watched many farmers plough and sow
Many crops have been harvested
while you stood as guardian there
and the land-owners, now long dead

A fine ornamental garden, terrace of yew
and 1930's Deco house was built
which waited eighty years for you
Having carefully renovated orchard garden
and tastefully extended the house
The dead oak was a danger to children
Big brother, Martin wishes to fell a tree
I, thinking it was a fruit tree, replied
"Sure for Amber, it's no problem for me"

continued

When I saw it, reaching for the sky
seventy feet high, perhaps more
I thought this is dangerous, I might die
Measuring the trunk in metres, I wince
It is enormous. I carefully cut wedges
on three sides, after attaching a winch
Martin and I took turns to cut it through
That heart of oak was tough as steel
we invited each other, final cut me or you?

I got the honour for the final cut to do
and as the tree top trembled
Martin at me, lumps of wood he threw
One more touch of the chainsaw blade, then run
Another thwack on my back, it's going, he cried
We ran to the chorus of cawing rooks, Its done
Creaking, cracking crashing down through trees
Banging, booming echoed down the quiet valley
Tea and cake arrived to stop the shaking knees.

COOL OR DEAD

Do you think it's cool to smoke?
Emphysema is one bad result
You slowly drown and choke
In your own fluids in the lung

I watched my father cough and choke
But you will argue that, he was old
My friends, one a really handsome bloke
have died, they were very young

continued

Graham, a handsome man, fifteen stone
brought five men down, laid out cold
Ciggies brought him down, sadly died alone
He thought he'd be alright, on fags he rolled

Three uncles have died from smoking tobacco
One had cancer protrude from his chest
Jack thought Pipe smoking best, went to rest
Harry had a had a ciggy holder, he joined the rest

Note. Fag is an English slang word for cigarette. When in Philadelphia, my eldest son Bernie was in a bar when he said to the local men. "I'm dying for a fag", He could not understand their response, until he was told fag was American slang for homosexual.

SMOKERS

Why do smokers think
it is other people's job
to sweep up dog-ends?

IS IT SLOW?

A slow worm
Try and catch it
It's very fast

LOVE AND MARRIAGE

Man's interest in a subject, woman or beast
is shown by his inventive titles, love's the least
Love turns by anagram into vole
it can often disappear down a hole

Love is not sex, sex is not love
True emotion flies high, a cut above
Pop songs of love, like a desert, fall flat
devoid of high feeling, who wants that?

Most modern songs cannot show
the true taste, of how love can grow
In a marriage, a joint venture to tread
trouble shared, lifts the heavy head

This is where you will find loves highest peak
But it is not a path that all men will seek
Some dream of loves lost in the distant past
or dream of tying virgins to their ships mast

True love will like waves, surge up and down
you must ride the turbulent sea of love or drown.

Note. Love is not a smooth easy journey.
But the journey is always better than the arrival.

GIVE A DOLLAR, BUT...

If you give a dollar, to a poor beggar or hobo
he will hate you because you have the dough
Strangely you will find your kindness
often repaid by actions that are mindless
If you wish to give, do not make a big show
do not place yourself where, I say "Told you so"

BIO-DIVERSITY

Meeting to save biodiversity of 193 countries
Japan agrees to save endangered species
but when will they stop killing whales

Not until they stop eating sushi.

PUT THE FUCKING LADDER BACK

My daughter asked me to trim a tree outside her motorcycle shop.

She borrowed an extension ladder
With saw in hand I climbed up high
Then slightly shaking, dismounted
height has an effect on my bladder

"Can you hold the ladder," I said
to a man standing there idly, idling
He was strong, about five foot two
I did not think, to test his head

continued

I climbed up high, and sawed away
and being timid, linked my elbow
around a branch, there were rocks below
“Cutting the same branch”? you may say

Without warning the ladder fell, far out
I hung on by my elbow, Oh, Oh Wow
He just stood there, looking at me
“Put the Fucking ladder back”, I shout

Still standing, looking, still, immobile
“That is really something and quick
for a man of seventy-four,” he quips
“Put the Fucking ladder back”, I said, in bile

I descend, thinking, He has a lack
of common sense or understanding
of someone’s imminent danger,
That’s why he didn’t put the ladder back

ABILITY

Females can catch fish
as well as a fisherman
A King can catch crabs
as well as a commoner.

Haiku 5-7-5 Syllables.

DANCE OF THE LEOPARD SLUGS

The most beautiful dance
You will ever see
Are two hermaphrodite slugs
hanging from a tree

Climbing the tree to a height
then out on a branch
They both entwine around
each other in a loving trance

Then as one they seem to fall
but are suspended on a slimy cord
A performance of a sexual embrace so complex
it makes you believe in our Lord

As they cling and spin around, a white umbilical,
looking like a silvery worm
comes out from behind their heads and join
to transfer to each other, their sperm

As they twist and turn, glued together
in a magical transformation
A white parasol is created to shelter
under, while in this act of procreation

Finally feeling complete, replete, they retract
their cords, then drop from where they hung
To depart forever, separately but not alone
as each one will bear and raise their young.

Note. I saw a program on TV about Leopard slugs.
I was stunned by the beautiful sexual act of these slugs.

THE WARNING

Red Berries abound
Curtains of golden leaves
Hard winter ahead

STORMS

Winter brings suffocating snow and slippery ice
Storms can and do come in many forms
Hot summer hurricanes are never very nice

A storm at sea is frightening to see
watching waves pile up then pound the prow
It's when on land, you desperately wish to be

Ripping the canvas of your sails
waves come crashing over the bows
as the wet wind howls and wails

Tornados terrify townships without hinder
Searing, scoring, scattering a path
turning terraces of timber houses into tinder

Hurricanes harass and harm country and city dwellers
as their property and possessions are pulverized
While some can remain safe in subterranean cellars.

PALS AND PUBS

I thought my life was quite normal
But now I am not too sure
I've never had a long-time friend, a pal

Was it because I never got drunk
or as I preferred female company,
I'd never choose to be a monk

I found most males moved with the money
So when things got tough, they flew
like bees searching for the pot of honey

I've organized companies, café's and clubs
planes, boats and balloons. But in times
of stress they all disappeared to the pubs.

AN ENGLISH WOOD

Autumn sun glows on the trees
Tasteful yellow brown colours, hues
I am such a lucky man to be
able to see such wondrous views
At first glance, empty very
quiet, dull, devoid of life
But on observation you will see
activity, change, peace and strife

continued

In this idyllic country scene
danger is there every day
A magpie dives and scatters birds
then struts in piratical black array
The jay his coloured relative
swoops and frightens the finch
It all looks like fun, but
It's their food, he will pinch

In apparent solitude, and peace
dewy grass is eaten by the hare
Silently an object drops and
five feet up, talons out, wings flare
A life has gone, once quick then dead
just a thump, flying feathers, a squeal
On the ground, just a fluffy tuft of fur
the eagle has taken home her meal.

Note. As this eagle dropped from the sky, I had thought it was a football until it opened its wings as airbrakes. It was a very large eagle with about a four-foot wingspan. It must have escaped from a Raptor Centre

INTERNET Haiku, 5-7-5 syllables

When dating take care
That sweet looking face might hide
a devil, tread with care

THE TROTTER. 2020

Kler-lop, clop-clop
He trot's, his hoofs make a rhythm
that is musical and constant

Occasionally on the tarmac road
there is a clippity-clop
as the trotting horse slips

As we come over the rise
the horse sees the descent
and slows without command

Holding back the two wheel cart
with apparent ease
with two riders, and no brakes!

On the flat, the driver speaks
very quietly to his horse
"Let's go" I feel the power surge

The huge thigh and leg muscles
tighten, the head lowers
and we surge forward, faster-faster

"How fast can he go" I ask
"Oh he is in third gear now"!
"30 miles an hour", I'm shocked

The musical rhythm of his pace
does not change, it just hums
It is sweet music to my ears

Cars, people and dogs pass by
This horse does not worry
hesitate, shimmy or shy

continued

He is listening to his driver
his owner, his friend
The caring relationship can be felt.

He does not need to be told
to go slow, down the hill
or power his way uphill

We stopped at the local Pub
A Guinness and a Latte Coffee
I was teased about my big blue hat

On returning home, the driver
and wife care for this horse
as if he was their only child

We must have travelled 15 miles of
lovely country, I've not seen before
although it is on my house backdoor.

Unhooking the cart
stripping off the harness
then showering off the sweat

Tenderly rubbing him down,
while he chews contentedly
placidly looking down at you

He is handsome, tall 15-2 bronze colour
Long whitetail, gentle large brown eyes
Holds his head high, broad in thigh

He's tucked away, some energy used
all of us having enjoyed the trip
through the Surrey Hills countryside

FORTY SHADES OF GREEN

I'm lucky to be here, in this time
In between the World wars
In England's perfect clime
Could have been born in a third world country
suffering drought and starvation
never to enjoy the free world's bounty

I am blessed, three kids, one above the norm
Two boys and a girl
All married with children, grandchildren born
My father was strange, perhaps mad
Genes, hopefully I take after Mum
People don't talk about it, that's sad

Once I had Dumbo's ears and Pinocchio nose
Wearing three league boots
I became nine feet tall, head to toes
But this tall tale came to a sticky end
when the Cambridge Hospital Doctor said
"Unload your problems or stay around the bend"

What's the point of having lots of money
if you can't enjoy it. If you've gone barmy
If you've lost it, not wealth, gone funny
Girlfriend had to go and stone quarry
valued possessions and much more
I got a quarter back but was not sorry

continued

The lovely lady that was my Mum
Snow-White? No, her name was Alice
She used to call me Fidget Bum
I always hated flat land, boring terrain
disliked school, I am dyslexic, not dumb
My mum used to call me Butterfly Brain

When in a Valley, sun poking through the trees
I wanted to be climbing up' high up
on the hill, skirting those dangerous screes
When I was here, I wanted to be there
If on the ground, terra firma
I wanted to be up high, flying in the air

I have tempted fate, in falling free
Sky-dived a mile, that is when you find
you know what life means. 'To Be'
I have sailed, flown, crashed, sunk and swam
Prayed for my kids lives and mine
and lived a full life and still, here I am

Amongst flowers of bright shades and hue
with forty shades of green trees, in my view
Now fidgeting but happily sitting with you.

BAA-BAA BASICALLY

Basically, what does that word mean?
Basically, this is the information I can glean
Basically, a word that has no meaning
Basically picking up seeds, gleaning

Basically for a slow moving brain
Basically to think of the next word chain
Basically you don't know your basic matter
Basically you say basically before you natter

Basically it's frantically, thoughts in fear
Basically to gain time, to get thoughts in gear
Basically it's like this, do you know?
Basically I don't, I have to put on a show

Basically used by young sales persons all
Basically that's it, I am not a poet after all
Basically, perhaps you might think twice
or more than thrice after this good advice

WHO PAYS Senryu

Who's going to pay
Migrants crossing the Channel
They will stay, you pay

SEXY C

I love her, not too old, in her prime
Her shape is slim with curvaceous curves
When out with her, it's as if I've had some wine
She's all mine, well for a time

Using the most rather expensive oil
we wash gently in a soapy bubble bath
She is so responsive, I am devoted
I am the swordsman, she my foil

A bit of a fast older girl, this one
If I try to push her too far
she howls and growls in protest
The last was a bit pedestrian, dull, no fun

She takes me to quiet places
play classical music and blues
Try out our paces, I don't push hard
My wish is her command, see people's faces

Perhaps she is too fast for me
the bladder does not hold so long
When you are getting old it means
disappearing behind the nearest tree

When in her black clad leather arms, I gently slide
holding me tight, I feel very safe
If I treat her gently, as I should
the better will be the ride

continued

Shiny black leather is my thing
Luckily I have the key
that ignites the energy within
the smell, the feel against my skin

My last old girl had an aluminium head
It was not so very fast
When it got very hot, it seized
Now, in that one, I would not be seen dead

DID I FOOL YOU?

This old girl has a very attractive bonnet
Which covers a slightly, unsightly head
That doesn't bother me, when in those leather arms
You don't see the chair, when sitting in it

I do have a little trouble getting in and out
I kneel on the ground, get my head in first
Ease my arthritic hip into the leather bucket seat
You see my knees don't bend, and there is the gout

My son's got a 1.8 Turbo, with lots of clout
My car is a select Celica two-door Coupe
not so quick but better than a rude red Nissan
that makes him look and sound like a noisy lout.

HAWTHORN, WITH BLOOD RED BERRY

Beware those sharp spikes
Smell the summer blooms
when perfume pervades the heights.

The Northern Shrike
on the Hawthorn
Its prey does spike.

Note. I smelt the Hawthorn for the first time flying over it in a balloon
Test the sharpness of the thorn with your finger.

TALIBAN

Taliban want peace
No women in their Peace Talks
Women will suffer

THE LONE TRAVELLER

As the light faded, the gypsy asked to camp
but the villagers gathered, to clap and stamp
We have to stop, or my poor horse will die
without rest, grass and water. "No", they all cry
"We won't have you here, lazy, work-shy
Gipsies, people like you, go away, goodbye."
Then she rode by; clippity clop. Does not dress up
or sat hunched like John Wayne, sits straight up

continued

Head held high, hands and reins held down
always smiling, I've never seen her frown
She's never haughty, or shows distain
for mortals down on the muddy terrain
Her dog, a scruffy, muddy terrier
could not be happier, merrier
Sitting still, on the rider's lap,
appears to smile, doesn't yap

Her bay mount, as cars pass by
does not worry, shimmy or shy
This lady has a natural rapport
apparent to all people rich or poor
This is, not only gained by being taught
but by observation and careful thought
The rider wheeled her fine steed around
studied the group milling on the ground

Then, "Follow me young man", she loudly said
To her large village house, the pair she led
Next morning he tells her, "I am not a gypsy
I'm creating a film programme for the BBC".

Note. She placed the Gypsy caravan on her lawn opposite the Golf club. Had he been left alone on our caravan site he would have been totally out of sight from the villagers.

GOODWILL Senryu

Generosity
Is so often mistaken
As being foolish

THE ROMANI

He's a true through and through Gypsy
is very strong and also quite tall
His perspicacity and powerful personality
is much bigger than us all

Born in a horse drawn caravan and
as a child he slept and lived underneath
Parents travelled for work farm to farm
In the winter they lived upon the heath

Picked potatoes, hops and all types of fruits
Stacked corn sheaves, children never came to harm
Cooked hedgehogs in clay, to hold the spines
Baked potato in ashes, al life with charm

Trousers held by leather belt and braces
on his head always wears a brown trilby hat
Big brown highly polished leather boots
He is tough, a softy really, wouldn't kick a cat

Didn't learn to read and write but take care
He might give you a sharp sideways kick
Not with those expensive polished boots
A quick wit and tongue does the trick

Has a great passion for trotting
An expert on horses, types and welfare
I had tears when his horse was hurt
and saw his heartfelt emotions and care

THE TALIBAN MAN

How honourable and brave is the Taliban man
that shot three girls in a stationary van
He had selected the fourteen year old
Malala Yousafzal for her views and what she told
She had declared that all girls should be educated
They in their wisdom, decreed she should be eliminated
I don't understand how the leaders or any man
can praise or condone this action of the Taliban

Pakistan 9th October 2012.

FISHING

With all the right gear in place, you wait
and wait, with hook line, sinker and bait
You know he is out there somewhere
you have the allure and lure, to snare

Hair coloured, eyebrows plucked, lids lined
ready to be escorted, fine wine and dined
The hook, the net, is in your good looks
you did everything by the woman's books

A pinned tongue, does not, clip your lip
clothes carefully crafted with tuck and nip
A big fish is what you want, so wait
A tiny tiddly one, is only good for bait

A flatfish, his poor nose out of joint, a plaice
or an elegant skate would not be out of place
But throw back the sluggish, big fat dud
with whiskers, that feeds in the mud

continued

You should ditch those with a slippery feel
dump overboard any aggressive conger eel
The one, is out there, treated with care
sometone you and your family can share

Should you snag a shark, do not play
because you will rue it forever and a day
Perhaps then one fine day, you will shout
I've caught a tasty fish, like a rainbow trout.

HAPPY DAYS

Happiness is not exclusive
to the famous and the rich
In life there is often a hitch
Happiness is there wherever you live
I've been happy just digging a ditch

THE RIDE

He was my little nephew, a smart young Tyke
He had his first motorbike ride on my big bike
I frightened him on this, now I call it a hack
Not realizing that one day, He would pay me back
Scene, my nephew arrives at the house. Say's "Hi"
Had not seen him for a while, he's now a big guy
Robert, I see you have a shiny new, red bike
Uncle, I'll take you for a spin, if you like

continued

His gleaming, red toy stood there quiet and tame
I had not seen the 1200cc engine or the name
I put my arms around his quite slim waist
Strange, holding on to men is not my taste
not realizing, I'd have to hold, with all my might
We started quite gently up Botany Hill
The engine's tone giving me such a thrill
My thoughts turned to my old 650 Triumph

We cruised past Crooksbury Hill and on
I looked at passing trees and setting sun
The sun through bare trees acted like a stroboscope
Flickering on my eyes, my brain could not cope
But now my attention has been diverted
We must be doing 110 mph to Elstead
Blind left-hand bend, house drives un-seen
I dig his ribs; I'm scared, I loudly scream

Slowing slightly, I know this road said he
I thought you had nerves of steel Uncle B
We rode through Elstead on to Rushmoor
This is nice; I said no need to rush any more
But uncle, you a Para and Balloonist all
I looked up to you, like you're ten feet tall
Oh, dear here's the Rushmoor two mile straight

I don't know what speed we did attain
past cars that seemed 'parked' to my brain
Tilford arrives in an adrenalin induced high
looking sort of gold and shiny, I'm glad the road is dry
Robert could feel my quivering arms and belly
Feeling pity or remorse, he then drove home sedately
with reduced velocity and engines tuneful hum
He said you're on a 1200cc Suzuki Bandit; chum

continued

I had thought it was a 600cc; not a Big Bandit
Home at last, I need a cup of tea and to sit.

Note. He drove at over 100mph down the Rushmoor straight which has a 30mph speed limit. Robert told me later that it was pay-back, because when he was a child he was frightened of flying. I tricked him into getting into my aircraft and took him for a flight. Not long after this motorbike ride, he died from stomach cancer. Robert Theobald, a really nice guy. He remains firmly and fondly in my memory.

FEEDERS

Feeding a person until they cannot walk
Rise from bed or pass through a door
Should be an offence under the law
Force feeding a goose for 'Pate de foie gras'
is illegal in some countries and states
The feeder is at fault for the problem it creates
You would be definitely charged with neglect
If you starved your dog, child, partner or kin
because you liked them as just bone and skin

WIND Haiku

Soft bodied people
must always hide underground
when hurricanes come

FELLING -FALLING -FAILURE

I studied the scene
then cut a vee in the tree
It fell the wrong way!

Haiku 5-7-5 Syllables

LET WOMEN RULE THE WORLD

Do not worry, you macho men
They will not desensitize
your favorite precious part
Women have more common sense
They are more creative in love and art
In nature males just fertilize
then doze, pose and preen
while their mates raise the offspring
Does this strike a note with you, a cord?
Have you noticed a familiar ring?
I have seen eloquent elegant
women speaking on rights
of people in dire state and need
silenced bypassed and ignored
We have had our strong women
In the past, Queen Victoria, Boadicea
and women pirates on the high seas
You might not have the physical strength
but determination and will power
can make men shake at the knees.

BLOOD RED RAIN

Blood red cells fell from outer space
maybe marking the end of the human race
Falling in the rain from the sky
Coming from a meteorite then did multiply
Upon Sri Lanka this red rain did fall
and mystified and terrified one an all

Scientists did later find to their chuckles
the red rain looked like blood corpuscles
A meteor had hit Sri Lanka weeks earlier
It acted like an intergalactic bulk blood carrier
Chuckles faded when they studied their find
The cells divide; is it a danger to mankind?

A true tale.

A MOAN ABOUT THE DRONE

Silent, Some-times a soft moan
from the rotary engine of the drone
When the intention, is to be known

Usually flying two miles high
above cities, unseen in the sky
but seeing all, as it passes by

Darkness does not stop its flying
infrared, night sights keep it prying
Sees through cloud, but thieves keep trying

continued

It scans truckers, tracks car trackers
immigrants and coastal smugglers
town muggers, even cattle rustlers

Don't think it will ignore little honest you
Car tax, Insurance evasion, planning too
checking extensions for Rates, and view

Even your holidays will be watched
Your average speed and travel clocked
in pretense of being Green, money docked

Speed, and travel miles clocked, what for?
In pretense of law and order, to tax you more
Even shopping will be watched, like Orwell's 1984.

Note. Did you think the drone was only for military use?

VARGAS LEGS

I saw Vargas pictures on E-bay this day
I was ten years old in the artists hey-day
Then I searched all my life, you will laugh
for those long legs belong to a Giraffe
Men fantasize, but they do not exist at all
as she would have to be eight foot tall

LEMMINGS IN A FINITE WORLD

Written in the year 2014.

When countries outgrow their living space
they fight wars and enter the Space Race
Looking to populate another world or planet
government cannot run this one, can it?

Who will be first to leave Earth, to flee
I am sure it will not be you or me.
World leaders have ships or yacht at sea
and sit in high ivory towers for all to see

Ships can sink and high towers do fall
Observe past lessons, keep green, keep small
Melting ice-caps reduce the weight at the Poles
to counter-balance Tectonic plate movement evolves

The world is not perfectly round you see
and it will adjust mountains and the sea
If you lived on a raft with food from Heaven
and would sink with more people than seven

Would you breed less, to balance the weight
or throw someone overboard, to re-create
Easter Island used up resources, couldn't live on kelp
their stone idols and priests could not see or help

As each nations wealth collapses down
people seek help in the nearest town
Farming slows, farmers cannot stop thieves
people begin to starve, eating dirt and leaves

continued

The young, with little ties, and their health
start to travel for food, shelter and wealth
It is my human rights they cry
as they rush and crush and sometimes die

The world already suffers over population
Politician's talk about saving their nation
The problem is each is saving his own skin
they do not seem to worry about kith and kin

More factories, more oil, more, it is a race
The elite buy islands for their private space
Life's normal brutal lines of population control
have been closed, now have a baby on the dole

It is not the end of humans just yet
but we will follow the dinosaur soon, I bet.

MINING ASTEROIDS

Mining asteroids does not seem
to be fiction or a distant dream
When the technology is firmly in place
If an asteroid threatens the human race
the company will be very profitable
that the asteroid threat it can disable

FARNHAM SURREY

Farnham was once a farmer's market town
they brought their sheep and cattle to sell
All such wonderful sights and country smell
Years ago it was called Fernham
because of the abundant ferns that grow
They are still there in parks and hedgerow
Just leave your land untouched
and the ferns will quickly spread
If the animals eat it, they will be dead
The Monks created Frensham Ponds
for fish, it took many years of toil
They built roads and cultivated the soil
living in seclusion in Waverley Abbey
where they farmed the land and did pray
Also managed the waters of the River Wey
imported fine furs from Russian traders
carried in bales up the river Wey by boat
Traded, bred cattle sheep and goat
They became too powerful for Henry VIII
and he required money for his wars
He stole their wealth and closed their doors
Down the river, Tilford with its Roman bridges
a ford where children swim, it must be seen
They have a cricket pitch on the village green
Then move on to see the Devils Punchbowl
where a highway was removed for you
so you can peacefully enjoy the view.

A SAD SENRYU Year 2015

I predict that drones
Will very soon be flying drugs
That is a sad thought

PERUSING POO

Perusing poo is a funny thing to do;
Have you thought to study, and peruse Poo?
I will never, pass over a drain without thinking
It might be stinking, but we went down
into the sewers of beautiful Brighton town
to study what people once did and doo-doo

The sun was bright, there was no rain
a cloudburst in Hove on this day
And we could be swept right away
like in the past, they could not be arsed
when everything went in the salty sea

Trusting that not too many bathrooms
have the bath plug pulled, or the chain
Or there is that storm of torrential rain
accelerating contents of each thunder box
swiftly sending me slithering into the sea

I have swum in muddy murky waters
and have been called a tardy turd
Not the worst word, I have heard
I have no desire to drink or drown
or be propelled in pee to Peacehaven Town

continued

From 1895 a semblance of sorting showed
Unless the storm drain overflowed
then all the Aristocrat's horses crap
ended up, or down on the sitters lap
of those that sat, on the foreshore shingle

There is a pretty portentous palace here
where a portly prince partied in his palatial pile
He had a tunnel to the beach, what style!
This to avoid the hoi polloi, the common herd
Then he swam unwittingly in their pee and turd

Our party, popping out of a Person-hole in a Park
caused puzzled pedestrians, pensive pensioners to
think, why, some young and pink, others old and pale
should participate in perusing poo, and gaily regale
their friends of this tale, they must be Nincompoops.

THE ROMANCE OF RECYCLING

My wife and I enjoy re-cycling it is good for the soul
Helps the environment, stops it going in a big hole
We've a site for caravans so they can roam
Then we sort their rubbish when they go home

But I am starting to get the hump
because we have to go down the dump
It makes me muscles ache and old bones creak
carrying and carting garbage every week

continued

Sifting, sorting the rubbish, plastic and paper
separating the bottles and tins for recycling later
Remains of food on our hands, covered in mustard
It stunk, then realized it was young baby's turd

Sorting out the paper, cardboard and plastic is fun
until I found little bags of what their dog had done
The dump sign said, 80% has not gone to landfill
I expect it's gone to Bangladesh to build a rubbish hill.

Note. Bangladesh gets a lot of flooding so it might end up being beneficial.

I HAVE 90 SECONDS TO LIVE

Please give the kids my love
ask them to forgive, mistakes
I've loved, and love you my wife
I have no regrets at all,
We've had the most fantastic life
You have been, and are my light
It was a lot of fun, some bad
things were done, can't alter that
I am sorry, we cannot have
a debate, a nice long final chat.
Aaargh. Amen.

A poetry competition

GOING POTTY - GOING MAD

I am going to tell you, I went mad
Now I can laugh and joke
At the time of being potty, I was sad
Thought I was clever, like all pushy males
Three businesses, Café, Bakery, in the South
A stone quarry up in the Yorkshire Dales

Married with three kids, liked to roam
Girlfriend in a Yorkshire town
She wanted me to stay, to set up home
Wife was unhappy, like men of the time
I was a male chauvinist pig
I thought all the choices, were just mine

When I married my father said to me
"A wife is a chattel". "What is that"?
I asked, "A piece of furniture". I agree
Home after building a new quarry factory
Watching T.V. Phone rings, Partner said he dropped
A fifteen ton block. Through the new roof actually

Said "Jim, was underneath", I thought he was dead
Putting the phone down I watch Disney World
I ask my wife, "Are my eyes popping out my head".
My ears are growing, like Dumbo's. He flies
"Oh, shut up", she sharply replies.
"My nose is growing, like Pinocchio's when he lies".

continued

I stand and stoop, I'm nine feet tall, see my wife's intrigue
Stepping like a trotting horse, with Jules Verne three league
Boots. Puzzled because I can only step one small league
In the Hospital, I shudder, maggots over me crawl
Doctors said "He is on drink or drugs".
Wife say's "He does not do either of that at all".

Soon after she said, "I'm going." It is late." I replied
"To go out this night, it is now half past eight!!
"You misunderstand I am leaving you", she sighed
Solution, Sold the Quarry at a loss, agreed divorce
Left the girlfriend, to start all over again
Wife was happy; kids were too, there was no remorse

EMPATHY

I saw a man, on a bright sunny day
wearing blue pyjamas, outside the
Guildford Hospital entrance bay

He was attached to a small trolley
and was watching a crane lifting
Building materials off a large lorry

Excuse me, I hope I am not too rude
but I am curious about you smoking
while attached to a trolley and a tube

Why's that plastic tube up your nose
I have only seen a person
on a TV drama, with one of those

continued

He said, "I was dying for a smoke
I am being fed by this tube. I have
throat cancer." I said, You poor bloke

Looking up towards the wards, he nods
"You want to see the patients up there
some are in terrible state, poor sods."

MONGOL TACTICS

Speed, mobility, hatred, systematic destruction
Street by street, block by block, total demolition

Square metre by square metre, tree by tree
leaving a desert as far as the eye can see.

Access, asset acquisition starvation, brutality, fear
All done without a care of a mother or child's tear

Control of food and water, power and aggravation
Deprivation, weakening the will of the population

Assets removed and sold including machinery
Banks controlled, trading in shares and currency

Hatred, jealousy, envy and greed are drilled
to have the required killer mentality instilled.

Note. You will recognize these tactics.

ASKING FOR IT

While in a Tesco store the other day
I saw something that caused me dismay
A woman was providing an unusual view
while standing at the head of the queue

The longest legs I've ever seen
in sheer stockings with shiny sheen
But what was it that made me gape?
High heeled shoes extenuated the shape

Women, old and young shook heads in disapproval
there is a limit in flaunting assets after all
A second good look revealed the reason
she did not have any hot pants or skirt on

Mind you I am not complaining
only telling you about it and explaining.
Wearing tiny green knickers, showing every shape
she is asking for trouble, abuse, attack or even rape.

Note. After my first glance, I wondered why the women in the queue were Tut-Tutting and clucking.
So, I took a second long look!

GROWTH

Growth can be obtained by war and Internet stealth
or gained by stealing mother earth's mineral wealth

It can also be won by improving a countries health
or lost by living in humans industrial waste filth

Perhaps lost by a nations people getting grossly fat
then having a Gastric Bypass, what is the sense in that

Westerners have less babies with future-plans laid
Many countries people bear children while on Food Aid.

Less children is a requirement to survive as a Nation
for with increased population there will be starvation.

THE BRITISH BAKED A BIG PIE

The government opened this pie
so the birds began to sing
"Give us money and houses"
This was their plaintive cry

I used to be British through and through
proud to fly the flag for me and you
Now I submit with regret
that's no longer how I feel, it's true

continued

Everything is upside down, right is wrong
Burglars get compensation if hurt or held
House owners get charged if they fight
Police then get a medal, called a gong

I have seen migrants get council houses
in week's, my family waited twelve years
Pensioners lose hard earned pensions, then
have to rely on children or elderly spouses

Jack and Jill climbed up High Street hill
to fetch a bucket of water, when she fell
Lawyers claimed compensation for her
she got a penny, after paying their bill

Some of our fellow human species
escape all this, passing into oblivion
Dulling their senses, fantasizing
through Booze, Coke, Hash and E's

Now don't get despondent about all this
Just get all the nations to work together
Reduce population by consent, not war
or freeze yourself into cryogenic bliss

MARRIED LOVE

Love and compassion
necessities, not luxuries
with-out them, love dies.

Senryu

HOT & COLD (Adult poem)

Have you ever chased
a naked lissom lady
through deep pristine snow
And felt hot blood course
your body in a burning glow

We climbed the mountain
across snow with icy crust
It was a sunny winter day
We were on a slippery slope
both with an intent to play

I chose a very peaceful spot
She was hot, snow so cold
We were not too young or old
Was it love? Perhaps or just lust
I will just let the story unfold

We were both bare, without a care
she lay beneath me, loving me?
Laid on the deep icy cold snow
she did not complain or cry
I never asked, I will never know

For every action, there is a reaction
and here was no exception
As we started to play
With arms outstretched she slid
off downhill, very quickly away

continued

She looked like a shooting star
as she cried out, Au revoir
Where she went, nobody knows
Leaving me with just a memory
and a bag of her 1960s clothes.

23/June/1966

MASTERS OF THE SKY

Eagles, they are masters of the sky
with amazing eyes that can see
a mouse or mole from one mile high

Utilizing an invisible power
soaring effortlessly in lazy circles
Notice they don't soar in a shower

They float on rising bubbles of hot air
called thermals, heated by the sun
taking care, for they are not everywhere

They are masters of flight
Humans try to emulate them with
Para-gliders but cannot fly at night

It looks effortless to you and me
It requires some brain power
it is, knowing where to be

Every flick of a tiny feather
informs the eagle about the air
and the surrounding weather

continued

When humans soar in their craft
unlike the raptor they sometimes
get caught in a dangerous downdraft

Free flying eagles have a place, a role
As predators are necessary to catch pests
unfortunately for the rabbit, mouse and vole.

Note. A competition entry.

FLIGHT

When once you have tasted flight
You will always walk the earth
With your eyes turned skyward
For there you have been
And there you will always be.

Attributed to Leonardo Da Vinci 1452-1519.

COPYING A SEAL

I and my friend, Snowy Yewdell White
we're canoeing off the Isle of White
Now, a mile off Bracklesham Bay beach
Waves possibly three metres trough to crests
we really should have worn our flotation vests
and were in a double seat old canvas canoe

continued

Climbing, sliding down each wave very fast
Our fun and laughter was destined not to last
The canoe disappeared like a submarine. Gone!
Now sitting in the water each with a paddle
similar to 'Up the creek without a paddle'
Next wave spins them round like propellers

Discarding these now dangerous tools
on the next rising wave, felt like fools
No use shouting for help, a mile offshore
I took all my clothes off, faster to swim
asked Snowy to copy, he refused. Is he dim?
"My wife knitted this woolly jumper", he said

An hour of swimming in winter cold
I am quite sure I will not grow old
Snowy saw me sink out of sight, said goodbye
I thought there will be a funeral, flowers, tears?
What if they don't find me? I'm full of fears
the fish, shrimps and crabs will eat me;

Now some fifty feet from the steep pebble beach
Lots of people standing watching, out of reach
My arms and legs were frozen, can no longer swim
down to the sandy bottom, I slowly sink
My next breath will be my last; I think
twiddle my toes in the sand, then I look

I am moving sideways, waves sweep overhead
I recall a seal in Padstow Bay popping up his head
So, pushing with my feet, popped up to breathe
Each time I did this, getting nearer to the beach
The crowd watched but did not attempt to reach
My wife Ann, she could hardly swim, came in!

continued

Snowy landed a mile away, he went pasty-white
he never got over that swim, that horrible fright
I often think about him saving that big wool jumper
Ex-wife Ann was extremely brave to enter that sea
to cling onto the wooden groin and to rescue me
When a hundred persons waited for me to drown

When pulled safely on the beach, some stupid bitch
with a handkerchief, tried to cover my naughty bits
causing me to shout, "You would willingly watch me die"
"but will not let me rest and naked lie!"

Note. Copying a seal saved my life.
Snowy died of cancer not long afterwards; I do think that stress has a detrimental effect on a person's body. I met Snowy when he joined my parachute club British Skydiving at Thruxton.

He was a keen cyclist to keep his legs in shape; there was not a lot of fat in his body. He told me that many years before he was run over by a military Tank.When he screamed the driver put the tank into reverse and ran over the other leg!

LUCKY

I met a Russian at Stansted Airport
He was a really pleasant guy
He had lost an eye, so I asked him
about his loss, with a sympathetic sigh

His reply was, "I am very lucky
to have lost one eye,"
Astonished at this answer,
I pursued the question to ask "Why,"

continued

My friends, nearly all are dead
Afghanistan, a senseless war no less
If not dead, they are all quite mad with
drugs or drink, post-traumatic stress.

Note. He found employment here, has married.

FEEDING, BREEDING DISCONTENT

Be "GREEN" and buy a tree, for a certain fee
Spent to cut down jungle for the oil palm tree
The date palm plantations kill diversity
Save the Arctic wilderness, don't let it spoil
But gold is at $1600, for that, miners will toil
Spoil detritus from that and drilling from oil?

In Africa, UN tented camps, women still breed
A desire to increase their brood, a basic need
This means there will be ever more to feed
It's been proven that charity money given for aid
has gone on guns to fight when foreigners invade
So much more stringent measures must be made

Now empty your pockets to explore outer space
but it's all part of the military armament race
Ready for when our earth blows up without trace
Outer Space, once a pristine place, with a view
to increase the human race, by a select few
Dream and scheme, I'm sure it will not be you

continued

You are confined to your allotted tiny space
The population increasing at tremendous pace
until the military, not God will remove all trace
Thirty years exploration now will turn to rust
for what result? To question this is a must
Is that cost of value? While Africa turns to dust

Note. I notice that Blueberries and Blackberries are being flown to the UK from Guatemala and plums from Chili. Advocado's from Peru, is that ' Being Green'. Year 2014

A DISCOVERY

Vacuuming is a pain in the?
Posterior region

Note. I only found out after my wife got cancer.
Luckily she survived.

THE SOMME

Some don't realize that on this battlefield
The British generals should have withdrewn
and commenced the battle elsewhere
The Germans had a clear field of view
Over one million men died, mowed by machine gun
on these killing fields, our generals were to blame
The British had single shot rifles and bayonets
Their political leaders should have died in shame

FLY SPIDER FLY

She did not attend Architectural school
Can build a complex web, no trouble at all
A structure of artistic geometry
in a fine mist, a delight to see
No husband, no language difficulty
can have sex then eat him for tea
Doesn't pay taxes there's no expensive MPs
she can fly effortlessly over the trees
Humans have fridge-freezers, life is harder
she keeps live victims in a silken larder
When she desires to travel, she is able
to make with strength of steel, a cable
Can spin a line, not verbal like a wheeze
but a long fishing line, to catch a breeze
The kids, hers kept in a silk web cocoon
unlike our teenagers, sod off too soon
When she decides to leave the unruly nest
no passport, just when the weather's best
to fly. We manufacture complicated machinery
she just makes fine thread using methodology
With no set plot, or rent or rates to pay
standing atop a branch, on a breezy day
spins out a line from her large posterior
Her big bum, her spinner, very superior
This thread, floats away from her bum
wind overcoming weight, equilibrium
Then a gust will lift her up, to fly
If a swallow sees her, she will die
Can she enjoy the view, from the sky
sure, she has many facets in her eye
Would I like to be a spider? No not I
I do not want a diet of moth and fly.

STILL IS BORING

Still sunny days, hot boring burning sun
turning people to drink and drugs
Others engage in sport, adrenaline for some

There is no magic in a becalmed boat
the senses become dull, becalmed
Flowing movement keeps interest afloat

Sometimes it is nice to sit still
But being immobile makes you fat
and stiff, and can make you very ill

Motionless creatures have no interest for me
Movement always catches the observant eye
an albatross in flight over sea, a delight to see

Heavenly stars would be dull, and unseen
without their burning twinkle
Caused by cosmic dust moving in between

Perspicacious people potter in potting sheds
potting lilies to avoid getting arthritic legs
and ready to adorn next summer's flower beds.

Note. I am sure that if you retire to an island in the sun
With a house that is perfect, nothing to be done
You will end up at the village bar to chat and drink
Soon you will find you have lost the ability to think

THE CHILD

The boy's innocent smile
sparkling untroubled eyes
Made me pause, to think
about children for a while
when their minds are free

A wonderful period of life
free of cares and worry
Not knowing sad or bad
or about war and strife
Remember to cherish this time

TEASING TARA

She is a nice package, pretty and petite
Delicate hands, slim fingers, strawberry blonde
Has excellent manners, appearance tidy neat
Large false eyelashes, slightly oversize, flutter
Sending out signals from bright blue eyes
Like a Naval, Morse code shutter

Her mouth is not too large or small
but she has a problem with her tongue
One crooked tooth does not detract at all
Her tongue flicks out and side to side
showing her pierced tongue. It split!
She swallowed the pin. Will it stay inside?

continued

Her belly button has a jewel that is red
will the next thing be a nose ring
to attach a chain to, and then be led
To have tattoos and things that parents dread
pins and rings through nose and lips
and other regions to gain more Street Cred

She has peaches and cream flawless skin
but I am afraid that will not last
She smokes, causing sickness unseen, within
She has certificates for First aid and swimming
Her boss at Bikebearings.com says she's efficient
I wish that she would concentrate on long living

This young lady that is lucky to be so perfect
in form and health, smokes cigarettes
which will ruin her health, Tara, please reflect

CONSUMPTION Haiku

If the world consumed
like Americans consume
We would need three worlds

THE SILVER NECKLACE January 1980

Here is a present for our parting
Poor exchange for an engagement ring
Not of coveted warm metal, gold
Holding message of love untold

Cold glistening uncompromising silver
Like your affection, frozen into icy sliver
Silver gleaming like the falling snow
Reminding me of the girl I used to know

Lightly dropping out of my life, patterns make
Which compare with the intricate single flake
Eventually every flake will disappear, melt
And like painful memories, no longer felt

Leaving a droplet, this barren earth to bear
Looking like a lonely person's tear
A teardrop of very ordinary water
Saying, "Wish we had reached the Altar"

Note. After my 10th poem to her she contacted me and we married on the 23/May/1980

THE LONE WOMAN

She stood in the corner by the factory wall
Once very attractive, had held men in her thrall
Now slightly furtive in her movements, uneasy
she fidgets, hands clasping as if feeling queasy
Looking for the right man to ask
to satisfy her, fulfil her task
Her skin used to be a rosy-pink colour
now has a dull grey and yellow pallor
Her fingers tremble as she reaches out, grasps
A passing male's arm, her voice then rasps
What type of woman do you think I am describing?

Years of smoking, she could not shout.
Croaks, "Got a light boy, me fags gone out

MAN AND TIME

The Ice-man slept on the mountain alone
for 5,000 years in the glacier ice to show
his tattoos, Bow, axe and tools of bone
The Pharaoh after 3,000 years, a dried-up husk
despite his immense power and wealth
proving man comes from dust, returns to dust

The Bog man with his trimmed nails and beard
waited 1,000 years to show his pickled tears
Killed for ritual? Or because he was feared
Man's image in granite will turn to slime
making clay so smooth it can eventually
emerge in pottery in some future time

continued

A carving of a man, in stone, an image
can in essence, live in peoples thoughts
It is man trying for rebirth, to re-emerge
This image can stand in hard static mime
to be transported through people's minds
but will last for a flicker of galactic time.

THE GALAXY BUBBLE, HUBBLE CANNOT SEE

Can a virus living in a person's vein
imagine or ascertain that
his world is sitting on a train
Similarly this applies to a flea
as he migrates from head to head
that he is travelling on you or me

Thinking that this is a better place to be
not knowing that, on that night
He will be washed out, to eternity
Perhaps earth is just dirt in a bubble
in which galaxies form and swirl, in a
bath of bigger bubbles, unseen by Hubble

Humans will never see or attain
the final piece of the puzzle, for
galaxies will disappear down the drain
and will go down the wormhole
as our astronomers call it
but it is just the big bath plughole

A RUMBLE RUMBLED

If female fingers don't feel and fiddle
Then her fond feelings have flown and
she's found another fella to follow and fondle
Should she stop smoothing the sheets
while you soundly sleep and snore
she'll share secrets and simply score
with some-one somewhere, skin to skin
If your darling don't draw down the duvet over you
While you drunkenly doze on the divan day bed
She don't care if you're doped, dizzy or dead.

LAMPADUSA LANDINGS

I doan-a wann-a mak-a an excus-a
Last-a year-a over fifty thousand emigrants
from North Africa landed in Lampadusa

The government must act! if nothing is done
to stop this tsunami of people, it will increase.
Repatriate them or Italy's economy will be undone

There is a need for empathy and pity
but at this rate of illegal emigration
their numbers will soon fill a city

Already financial problems loom and a job shortage
and if this tide is not put under control
Italians are liable to rise in anger and rebel in rage

And all travel plans have unraveled

13/11/2012

AGE

Eighty is not fun
Being Ninety must be worse
is there an age pill?

THE TALMAG TRIAL

It's for British Bikes built pre-nineteen sixty-five
before all the foreign imports started to arrive
Only four stroke engines are allowed
not two strokes, they are far too loud
Minimum age entrant is sweet seventeen
maximum age, one hundred, never seen
Solos and sidecars all with twin shocks
The site is sandy gravel, no big rocks

There will be hairy blokes in Barbour Suits
with open helmets and big black boots
There are some women entries too
they will show the men a thing or two
by wearing the latest modern coloured gear
and smile and laugh, where men show fear
By belting up the gravel of Hungry Hill
standing poised on the pegs, giving all a thrill

The old men steadily pottering and muttering
around the course, engines often spluttering
Young ones blasting, roaring up and down the hill
some involuntary wheelies with spectacular spill
A sweet Castrol R oil smell fills the air
A male perfume, that's becoming rare

Listen to the roar of exhausts on twins
and heavy thump from Velocette fins

It is nice to see the various British bikes
polished aluminium engines of different types
This club event started seventy years ago
each year thousands of spectators enjoy the show.

Note. This event is held at Hungry Hill, Aldershot, Hants.

CHINESE FACE Senryu. My wife's face

I enjoy your face
When your smile brightens your eyes
my heart beats faster

AMOUR AND ARMOUR

When a young lady is looking for amour
in a man she can love for evermore
If she wears full body armour
It makes it harder to get ardour

She might have lots of good assets
like long auburn hair and other bits
Her house, it's a little log cabin and a car
and an old hound that does not travel far

continued

She sits alone writing poetry, she's well bred
Has warm brown eyes but crying's made them red
but travelling in a car or stuck in the old log cabin
a mansion or flat, or any other places you are in

The house, dog, car can stop the love, amour
It will inhibit men because it acts like armour
You need to leave the car and get out and about
there is no need to advertise, scream or shout

Join a social club, dance but take care with drink
Meet people, don't stand at the kitchen sink
There can be a danger in the world-wide Internet
friends on there are ethereal, they are never met.

Note. I wrote this in response to a very sad poem written by a woman that lost the man she loved.

HOLIDAYS

We all dream and wish
for the pristine beach
With clear clean water
and able to eat fresh fish
Lone couples cavort on the white sand
eat lobster with background of blue sea
This is what adverts continue to show
to the music of a local blues band
But when you have travelled
You soon will have learnt to know
The beach is covered in rubbish
the sea dark and polluted

THE FIERY FEMALE 13/05/1980

My wife is like a Roman Candle
She is very difficult to handle
Most of the time she sparkles brightly
then explodes mightily and frightens me
Like the firework that spits a pretty shower
then shatters the peace and makes me cower
Then as I head to the household door
She assumes the sparkle that I adore
Such is the pattern of a fireworks display
and ups and downs of marriage each day

MY WIFE THE ORCHID

The orchid was crushed on its journey
The last bud, showed its potential
Later it bloomed and showed its beauty
She never had a car or learnt to drive
We met, started giving driving lessons
I am very lucky to be alive

Left or right, she could not tell
My side or your side, I had to say
"you've gone up a one-way street" I yell
She was always ready to disappear
Money saved, and suitcase packed
At women I must not look or leer

Such a fragile state she was in
My raised voice could cause
a catatonic state to begin
Gradually as the years rolled by
Her stories emerged of brutal actions
and I understood the reasons why

Jokes, she could not understand
I thought it was all because
she came from another land
Carefully tended, this delicate plant
has flowered, a friend, a wife
Such a treasure I could not supplant

Her humour lost in years past, is there
Every day, a smile, some fun
Her tongue is sharp, so I take care

I love my friend, my pal my wife
The flower had been without humus
The humourless lady gave purpose to my life

BIRTH RATE Senryu

African birth rate
is the highest in the world
So they, immigrate

TWO ODDS MAKE IT EVEN

When I first met my Chinese wife
Pheromones made me wish to sire
she resisted my early advances
that I wanted, it was self-centred desire

She crumbled under my onslaught
of attention, letters with poetic line
eventually married, but still worlds apart
although Chinese and English genes are fine

She's smart, meticulous with mathematical mind
so was confused by my scruffy style
A war of words and different worlds
left us at odds for quite a while

On my first visit to her family
to ask for consent to wed
I put my feet on her lap, for her to massage
caused concern from family, conversation dead

Being hot and humid, she went in the shower
I joined her; common sense I did lack
she, conscious of saving water, agreed
Well, I always wash her beautiful back

continued

Two children, Wei Yeh and Kiki had watched us
by quietly laying on the floor
"Mummy, they are both in the shower,"
they cried, as they peeped under the door

She used to reproach and chide me
about being horrible and rude
now all she can complain about
is not squeezing the toothpaste tube

We have had a wonderful
forty-one years together
It was hard going, the first three
Now combined, birds of a feather

Note. Regarding feet in the fourth verse.
The Chinese regard the feet as very dirty and should be kept on the floor, not put on laps

RED ROSE- SHARP THORNS

I awake from a deep dreaming sleep
and hear sharp words from you this dawn
You are like a red rose with shiny dew
but I note the sharpness of the thorn

Please do not raise your voice to me
about an insignificant matter, a trifle
The best of me, the ultimate is
obtained by persuasion, not whip or rifle

continued

I look at you through sleepy eyes, its
not a question of you or me, it's we
I've said to you many times before
You do not know what you do to me

In our marriage and daily life
A raised voice, harsh words are no use
my early learning days were fraught
with shouting ridicule and abuse

We've been together many years now
Let us go about our normal purpose
and truth unfold, accept mistakes
adjust to others foibles in quiet repose

Note. In early days of marriage there will be differences in opinion
Quiet debate and discussion is the only way to resolve issues.

18/Dec/2009.

YOU CAN ENTITLE THIS

They thought it just and right to chase
to persecute, and prosecute Saddam Hussein

Now they help the Iraqis to fight for
independence with no financial gain

Unless later there could be benefits from
owning shares in the oil gravy train.

PICKING PETALS

She loves me
She loves me not
when anniversaries I forgot

She loves me
When I am ill, cares for me
Loves me not if I argue a lot

She loves me, cooks a lot
Loves me not when age
makes me forget the plot

She loves me
when I do the washing up
Loves me not when I bid on E-bay a lot

She loves me,
gives me pocket money
Loves me not when on my motorbike I trot

She loves me when I massage her leg
She treats me like a Faberge Egg
So she must love me

FELINE FUN Haiku

Do you value me?
Hubby, you're a lump of gold
an inert object!

HOT HOUSE

"Lots of things go off
in this house, milk, food," she said
I hope she doesn't mean me?

My wife told me off for leaving the milk
out of the fridge.

I WILL SMACK HER

My wife said, "I am allergic and not slender
My stomach is fat and very tender,
I cannot stomach, anything that is old
Preserved, ham, bacon, cheese with mould,"
It must mean, she is allergic to me, I'll smack her!

Note. She did say this, but I will not smack her, because the consequences would be dire.

TRUTHFUL LOVE

Old age is like the last page in a book
You don't want to see the end, but you'll look
I want to compose more poetry
Write a poetry book, perhaps earn a fee
It's time to show appreciation to my wife
She has shared all my troubles and strife

continued

We have been lucky with our health
Gained sufficient wealth without stealth
When I've been ill, she nursed me well
If I tried to lie to her, she could tell
I told her " You are a beautiful woman" her reply
"Inside or out?" Both I reply with a tear in my eye

"Why is it then, that only ugly males
give me the eye, lie and spin fairy tales
I have never attracted handsome men
"So, I am lucky to marry you then!"
"Oh, you are different, from what I've seen
I like being valued, treated like a queen.

RADIOACTIVE Senryu

Wife looks radiant
Radiotherapy treatment
ended this day

BIG BANGS AND BOSONS

Scientists at the Cern Hadron Particle Collider
said the search for the God particle was over
Before The Big Bang they say there was nothing
an explosion must be created from something
So that something? That was created
By and from what? That is not debated
Does space have a beginning or an end?

continued

Thinking of it can send you round the bend
A particle that gives atoms their mass
was Professor Higgs idea in an inspirational flash?
Apparently particles start with mass, like light
Collecting Higgs bosons and become heavy, not light
this will explain the missing quarter
of the universe, bosons being dark matter
It's taken fifty years to create this at Cern

The tremendous cost involved is my concern
If the Higgs boson is proved to be found
It will be Nobel prizes given all round
But if the newspapers declared one morning
It was not. Would you all go into mourning?
Will it help to manufacture food, to help feed
the millions in Africa, now in desperate need
The costs I know will keep on soaring
It could be spent on averting Global warming

I'd like cheaper fares on the train and bus.
Interesting science but of no benefit to us
What is the benefit to the common populous?
Good for scientists, not for me or you, us
It cost £2.6 billion, with 10,000 scientists
Now they are behaving like Oliver Twist's
They want £20 billion for a new collider
The old one will soon be on eBay for a fiver

November 2010

TURF WARS Senryu

With Global Warming
there are too many people
So, immigrants, wars.

UFO'S AND GOLDFISH

Like goldfish in a bowl, odd ones try
to jump out, fall back or die
Astronauts blast off, beating gravity
They don't fly back, they fall without levity

Think you understand gravity, you're a fool
UFO's understand it; they use it as a tool
Stop still, then accelerate with consummate skill
If humans emulated them, G force would kill

I kept quiet about it. I've known people put away
Don't laugh, think I lie, proof will come one day
A young girl in our village, put away for her good
for giving birth un-wed, it was called Brookwood

Brookwood Sanatorium, where lunatics were sent
or if you misbehaved or stole, was where you went
It was in the nineteen fifties, haven't pinned the date
Farnborough, Flying Bedstead was the time, I relate

Hiding from my father, one fine summer day
as teens are liable to do, laying in a field of hay
This was at Homefields, Runfold, Surrey
Puffy cumulus high above float past slowly

continued

Directly above me, passing West to East it flew
a silver Barrage balloon, I thought I knew
At Aldershot, Para's jump from these things
But wait no cables, basket, tail or wings

Circular, shiny grey, it stood above, quite still
The clouds were moving, no windows or grille
From dead stop, it sped, don't say floater in the eye
At two thousand feet, NNE it sped across the sky

Stationary balloon? In the wind, what was that?
Now disappears to the horizon in three seconds flat
No noise, smoke or contrail. Or death ray
I thought it was a secret plane, from the USA

Next day, Daily Paper, Flying Bedstead, all the rage
It was the Harrier Jump jet at its very early stage
I had the Observers book of Aircraft
what I saw was not a British craft

As the years passed by, U2's and Cold war lies
I assumed it must be one of those Russian spies
Seven others saw that thing, Police and Airmen
I have kept quiet all these years, they will come again.

Note. That UFO sped across the sky to the horizon, 20 miles in 3seconds, at the time I equated this to be about 3;000mph but knew no aircraft could do that. Now I think it was faster.
Humans are like goldfish in a bowl which get looked at now and again to see how they are getting on. This event took place 6/9/1950 and was seen by a Farnborough RAE Pilot. There was also an article in the Farnham Herald 25/1/2002 about it.

LANGUAGE

Derek Springate was a Parachute Regiment man
He said to me. “When I were in Arab Dessert
I painted my name on all t-toys
Whose toys? I asked. “No, the animals t-toise.”
He replies, with accent from the UK north
He put his name on all tortoises he found
His way to be remembered, this lovable tyke
Sadly, he hit a bulldozer when on his motorbike.

I met Derek when he joined the British Skydiving Club at Thruxton. He was stationed at Aldershot, Hants.

A NEW LOVE

I found a new love in the women I did marry
She was argumentative, but I did not tarry
I chased and besieged her, kicked on her door
Wrote her poems till she couldn’t resist any more
But she did not come to live and stay
she preferred her flat and to work away
Was she coming to live with me one day?
I asked. “Do I have to.” is all she could say.
“Oh, I love my flat, do I have to come?”
I think you should, and work as one
She did not falter as we walked to the altar
Thirty-two years married, I cannot fault her
Her loving is not in lust or passion
but her care and kisses are my heaven.

YES-M-BOY

When my father said to me, do it my way
or shut-up, I did, perhaps you'll see why
I had just left school, my job was cleaning bricks
Our house had burnt down, one of father's tricks
Employed by dad to help do the work
was a twenty year old, with tendency to shirk
I don't know why, but he was called Yes-me-boy
alias perhaps? About his past, he was very coy
One lovely summer day, with scented smell of hay
Dad called by, to give Yes-me-boy his pay
The nice young man, said "I want more cash,"
Dad retorted "You get free food, a room, cash, don't be rash,"
Y-M-Boy said, "If you don't, I'll tell Labour," Tax office he meant
Dad, quietly looked around, then slowly downward bent
picked up a galvanized one-inch water pipe, four foot long
Weighed it, then without a word, hit Y-M-Boys left leg, Bong!
Changing hands as Y-M-Boy started to sway and fall
acting like a cricketer, He hit his right leg like a cricket ball.
Not a word, not a cry, he fell, I worried perhaps he'd die?
Let's go, my father ordered. Three days then went by
On day three, police arrived in force, six or more
unceremoniously, they slammed dad to the floor,
Next, I am in the High Court, on the prosecution side?
The Barrister flew towards me, black robes flowing wide
"I contend that you are lying", (I'd never heard 'contend' before),
"You are keeping quiet, tell us what you saw."
"Nothing, I was on the other side of a shed." I glibly lied
Sobbing true tears, the Judge said, "Step down." then I cried.
Later it emerged that Y-M-Boy crawled to a roadside bay
Quarter mile at least and there, bleeding, unconscious lay.

continued

Bob King an A.A. man, found him, we called him Uncle Bob
Run over, he thought, did not know, who did the job
Yes-m-boy had tried to blackmail dad, which he did regret
Dad was acquitted; it is something I cannot forget.

Bob King was the AA's Pin-up man in the 1950s.
There was a 20ft high picture of him in Leicester Square London.

JUNK ART Haiku

There is a sickness
if a dirty bed is art
the art world is mad.

Note. The artist is just taking advantage of a stupid society.

HARVEY

This is to record from year one, of battles that you have won.

In this year you have learnt a lot
You learnt to move, to crawl
but too quick to stand, you fall
You learnt to drink from a cup
To use your teeth, to chew, yummy
Also learnt to manipulate your mummy
Why reflect on stuff that's in the past?
Why ponder where the moon has gone
Seeds grow where the Sun has shone

continued

Years tick away, far too soon
For children, time's too slow
they want to talk, to walk, to grow
Tick tock time does not stop
The wheel of time goes round
to which we all, are bound
Time for adults can alter, fast or slow
Too fast, while pleasure is gained
Too slow, when you are pained

This wheel of time goes in a circle
and every movement, every tick of time
Has an effect on you, me and mine
Is history a waste of time and effort
The world is just a ball, its round
and we and events go round and round
Life is a never ending play
and we all, have just a line
To see into the future, read mine

Stop and give time to look
for each life, each wing that flutters
will affect your life, and others
Enjoy each moment, each event
You will with wide eyes, record
to marvel at the dew on a spiders cord
Don't step up to manhood too quickly
Enjoy the child's delight and fun
sweets and treats and very sticky bun

continued

Teenage years will always be a problem
Mums and Dads don't always understand
when you want to stay late with the band
Danger will always be a part of life
cotton wool always feels the same
Adventure will sharpen wit and brain
Will motor bikes always be around?
They are not safe my mother cried
I wonder if your mum will let you ride

Touch is such an important sense
Give time to touch and feel
and father time might slow his wheel.

Note. This was written for my grandson,
Harvey Allaway's first birthday.

LONELY

She was far away
Sleeping in a single bed
Distance 6inches

Senryu

OH DEAR, ANOTHER YEAR

She is a cutie, she is pretty as a doll
smart enough to be a gangster's moll
She is a mother, secretary, coaches football
Taxi driver, cook, friend, advisor, she is all
She's not a young chick any more
but in a race, will be in the fore
She used her charm on the local island farmer
to repair her motorbike, which broke under her
she still came tenth in International Trials
Riding sidecar over many rough Manx miles
unlike me she never learnt to swear or curse
and now has become an excellent nurse
Which now that I am frightfully old
I let her tell me, to do as I am told.

Note. This is my daughter when she owned an Off-road motor-bike shop

TRUE PLEASURE

What is true pleasure
unadulterated joy
To come home each day

Senryu

WIFE FOR SALE

My wife is growing old
It's time that she is sold
I'd like a sweet young model, but then
in a few years she'd want younger men

I cannot pretend that my wife is a valuable antique
But thinking, I've long realized that she is unique
She is from the Far East, with soft silky brown skin
Her kindness and beauty is also hidden deep within

Today I saw this funny old man in the glass
of a shop window, I nearly fell onto my arse
I realized that funny old man, was me I could see
badly dressed and toothless. She might get rid of me!

I like wearing a vest inside out, it looks ugly it seems
but it's more comfortable wearing with outside seams
That is how a man can often look, act and be
rough on the outside, but soft inside you see

Young ladies might have the looks and sparkly eyes
But bland blank blondes' verbosity very often belies
I need my wife to spell, calculate and punctuate
She is a superb cook, literate, is timely, never late

Speaks the truth to me, hurting my masculine pride
At times told a little white lie when fighting by my side
A book with blank pages is boring and hard to read
To keep active, caring intelligence is what you need

So you macho men enjoy a look and then, think
Lawyers will have your money before you can blink.

A HUSBAND TO GIVE AWAY

I want a man that is not meek or a dope
that does not drink alcohol or smoke
With nice teeth set firm in each socket
not a set of false teeth kept in his pocket
A man that will carry his mobile phone
so I can keep in touch with him from home
Doesn't gallivant for hours or disappear
turning up to ask, "What's for dinner dear?"

Not someone that wants me to wear tight dresses
and would like my hair to be in long tresses
I'd like some cuddles and caresses now and then
before he disappears for hours into his private den
cleaning and caring for his precious motorbikes
or quietly composing poetry and stories he writes
But then I'm thinking that the one I've got
does not annoy or argue with me a lot

But I'd like a man that listened carefully to my advice
although I might have repeated myself twice or thrice
One that will occasionally cook a meal for me
and not forget my birthday or our anniversary
A man that will lock the door at night
not watch late TV, but to hold me tight
And a man that does not wear socks to bed
or cramp his style by a woolly hat on his head

continued

Nor to ride his motorbike too fast
because I want the relationship to last
Saying that has made me think about my hubby
he is not abusive, works hard, not thin or tubby
does not tell me how to dress or what to do
I have found him honest and too truthful too
we've had hard times but many happy years
Perhaps I'll keep him, I can't stand his tears.

FORTY TEARS AGO

Bradley and I, over forty years ago
were Bellboys on a ship, with P&O
He was my pal, a gentle guy called Brad
he got the blame for what I did, it was bad
At Port Side Egypt, boats surround the ship to trade
selling everything, fruit, handbags, things handmade

Traders in the bumboats throw strings up high
then in a basket you send money, they reply by
sending up your purchase, one did not, so I
dropped a 'rubber' full of water from 50 ft. high
It hit his boat, this blew all his goods into the sea
Later at the cabin water level porthole, he saw me

I quickly closed down the steel deadlight
After work when I returned that night
There Brad was, left and right black eye
he cried, "I was beaten, I don't know why
I heard a tapping on the porthole, and a shout

continued

A foreign chap grabbed, pulled my head out,
and punched my nose while holding my hair
Why he did that I do not know, it was not fair."

Note. Brad looked like a Panda Bear, I felt guilty, and I am very sorry for I did not have the nerve to tell him. I feel bad about that.

TIME

You are driving a car, half-awake
you see an accident, you brake
Time slows, when your life to preserve
you see vehicle positions, people to observe
Their faces, their places, the cause, the cat
crunch, slow motion impact, things like that
Time is governed by your brain's reaction
While it works out, your best defensive action
So when you and I turn to stardust
which is unfortunately a must
With no brain in what's left of you and I
A trillion, trillion years will pass easily by
Enjoy this journey; slow is better than direct
the destination might not be what you might expect

MALAYSIA

When as a Sailor, I landed in Penang
I loved this far eastern city
Little did I realize that I would marry
a Chinese girl living in nearby Kelang

My next port of call was Singapore
I watched the coolies working hard
amused to see their hairless legs
Then I met an attractive whore

"Call for a Taxi Mister Orang-puteh man"
As we walked along the promenade she
asked for a kiss, throwing back her head
I looked up her wide nostrils, then I ran

A food stall, it was ages since I ate
I felt at ease with these people as
I walked around the town alone
ate Nasi goreng without any sodium glutamate

Admired girls with black hair, wearing Cheong Sam
that showed sinuous curves of slim figures
It did not occur to me that my future wife
was probably in still in a pram

When I was serving in the British Army
she came to England as a nurse
In a restaurant she walked past me, I
became fixated to marry her, was I barmy?

continued

It took a hard year and more
to get her to say "yes" to me
We've been married forty years
I would like another score

She is my best friend and mate
she is like a mother hen to me
I think she is special, rather rare
I'm so pleased I asked her for a date

She is my cook, carer and advisor
We have had few tantrums and tears
and saved my life on two occasions
I could not wish for anyone wiser

Orang puteh means white person!

THE GREEN WOMAN Senryu

I am turning Green!
You're wearing a silk dress
reflecting sunlight!

A true story. This lady came to me with a genuine concern!
Her face had an interesting green sheen

MERCHANT NAVY, MY TOES

When young, in long evening hours
I wanted to develop special powers
and lit matches with my toes
Now it is useful as flexibility goes
Like movie stars Bond and Bob Hope
I imagined I was tied up with rope
then with my toes, got a match from a box
Of course, after removing both my socks
then lit the match using just my toes
I burned my bonds to elude my foes
These games with my stiff little toes
helps me now as my flexibility goes
to pick up pens, pencils, clothes and hankies
with both my feet, using those little pinkies.

Note. Evenings spent off duty in the Merchant Navy with nothing to do. After watching a Laurel and Hardy film in which Laurel waggled his ears. I concentrated and practiced wiggling mine. I can still do it to the amusement of small children. I later found out that it was done by studio magic.

CRY OUT

WARSAW GHETTO

NEVER AGAIN

GAZA.

Note. Politicians are constantly saying "NEVER AGAIN".

TEDDY BEAR, FORGOTTEN

Mother, please don't reproach me
I'm sure you have loved
He is everything to me, I feel free
he is my love, strong and clean
Wait until I'm older? Old men, you
do not know where they have been;

You are a mother, aren't you?
don't you understand?
I want to have children too
Control my sexual urge? Oh Mum
I've seen my peers party, swinging
I am happy with my one, only one

Look I could be behind the shed
doing it, even in the school library
but I don't, I keep it in his bed
I've been open with you, you're not Cupid
He will, I know work very hard
I'm fifteen remember, and I'm not stupid

I have it worked out, neat and pat
We will stay at his parent's house
until we've saved enough to buy a flat
I can work, if you will baby sit?
Your second car, he can drive
I'm sure that you don't need it

So, with her head in a whizzing whirl
of dreams of love forever
this young lady, lost being, a girl

This was for a competition.

NHS Haiku

Require heart surgery?
If you are obese or smoke
You might not get it

Think about it, as if you were a surgeon.

A NOBLE COUPLE

Sturdy, tall broad and strong
standing out from the throng
A row of sentinels in green by his side
he has spread his seed far and wide

She stands near, in red and yellow a fine array
it's custom for her to bear each year, to display
Tall, she swings side to side, bends and sways
looking good, but she has seen better days

Her young are close by, growing fast
sadly, this winter, will be her last
He has many fertile years ahead still in hand
guarded by sentinels marching across the land

Beautiful in her youth, her age quickly shows
disease sets in, her silver shine slowly goes
Her berries, like red cherries, to pick
Trees have red fruit, attracting birds to peck

continued

His broad limbs spread wide to gather the light
like arms held out to stop others gaining height
Woodpeckers drill her bark for bugs, fungi attack
winter wind brings this Silver Birch down, Crack

The large Oak planted by a squirrel for winter vegs
Stands protected from wind by the Lawsonia hedge
Which in soldierly serried ranks of evergreen
dull the autumn colours, simply as a screen

Note. Many Lawson's Cyprus trees have been planted in the UK for hedging. The indigenous fauna do not like them and birds will not use them for nesting.

POWER

I could hit you hard
with my fist, but if I missed
Better use writing.

Haiku.

MY YELLOW BRICK ROAD

I, like the Scarecrow, born without a brain
It was dyslexia, later people became aware
In my youth, the teachers just did not care

I tried to find the correct road to take
Sailed to Australia, the place called "Oz"
to find salvation with the Wizard of Oz

Searched for my personal protective Wizard
But only found an Aussie poisonous toad
and shipped back to England covered in Woad

Then I ducked, dived pranced and danced
skipped, fell, floated free and flew
Made few friends but enemies, quite a few

I possessed a strong heart, steel nerves
Suffered injuries, with lots of pain
Would have fared better with a brain

My Wizard, I found was not a man
but a woman, with a name of Lou
My wife, made all my dreams come true.

Note. I saw the film THE WIZARD OF OZ in 1940, of course I associated myself with the scarecrow man. He had very little brain.

MODERN GOLD RUSH

Millions in Africa require feeding, I am told
Haiti has many to shelter, events still unfold
Millions homeless and starving in Sudan, and Darfur
Pirates help themselves, so what's the Navy for?
Aid makes these people think, America is made of gold
There will be a price to pay for aid, watch events unfold

2015

YOUR BABY Haiku

Your child, boy or girl
Now 6ft tall and 200 pounds
is always your baby

MY NOSE

I have cured my big bogey nose
by thinking of an elephant's trunk
that he uses, like a water hose

As we were created in the salty sea
and like seals, have a nose, but they
don't seem to get clogged up like me

An elephant, through his trunk can drink
and then blow out a jet of water
so these two ideas, made me think

continued

Mixing a pinch of salt in a cup
dissolved in warm water, then
putting to my nose, sucked it up

Sweet flowers and roses, it was not
Now I have lost my nasal green garden
it's sad, and then perhaps it's snot

For now I can enjoy the smells of life
air flows through my nose. Best of all
I can smell the sweet aroma of my wife.

Note. A true blessing for me, but don't try this without obtaining your doctor's advice.

VOODOO

Forget scary vampires from Transylvania
there are far worse events now in Tanzania
In Africa, Witchcraft practice still lingers
Albino families fear losing life or fingers
Unbelievably stupid gold miners
are killing albino adults and minors
These miners believe in Witchcraft or Voodoo
and having an albino's flesh, wealth will accrue
While sadly the Government's actions are slow
the witches influence and activities still grow
They practice and kill in Satan's name
encouraging illiterates to maim for gain
Albinos in Tanzania are cut into little pieces
The predators are their folks, the same species.

MARTYR'S LETTER

Here, my train of thought is in despair
I am in prison, although in fresh air

Held by a section of the human race
never ever being, face to face
Bombs being dropped on me and mine
I will dig a hole, tunnel, plant a mine

If that does not allow me to escape
reality, peace of mind or this fate
I may as well be dead, this life is a bind
thoughts cross my mind, I will find

a dud shell they dropped, has explosive
I will be a human bomb, don't wish to live
Then, I will be remembered ever after
anonymous untill then. Yours from Gaza

SUCCESS

Don't judge success by the friends you have,
But by the enemies you've made.

THE DEEP DIVE

When my wife went abroad.

My love for you soared like a singing bird in a cloudless sky
Your absence plunged me down, a wreck in the still depths to lie

I felt like a denizen of the deep that of sunlight was not aware
Stillness where your sunlight could not reach, to heal my despair

The quiet was not disturbed at all by passing of boat or craft
I longed for your voice to speak to me, to give me a life-raft

Your smile came, a shaft of light, like on the seabed does show
allowing the plants to flower, and my love for you to grow

THE CYCLIST

Today, driving up from behind
a cyclist in front of me, I note
She had a trim figure, firm behind

Wearing cotton top, very thin
lycra shorts, helmet, bare arms
No gloves, a pale unmarked skin

A nice sight to observe, to see
but she is living dangerously
Most probably unwittingly

continued

Legs pumping gracefully, and fast
slender, uncovered, no knee guards
The cars still squeezing to get past

No mirrors, she doesn't look back
her life is in the car driver's hands
Only their care, prevents a whack

I do hope she does not crash
and spoil that perfect figure
Or mark her skin with gravel rash

I never looked to see her face
I care because she is young
And is of the human race

I'd like to give her one,
of those inflatable safety bags
or a set of proper cycling clothes

TIME CAN CHANGE

If time stands still
Minutes seem like hours
It is possible, you might be ill
When time speeds up and passes by
You must be content, in love, well fed
with no reason to worry, fret or cry
Sometimes time can stop or slow
freeze framed, picture frame by frame
This in accident avoidance, adrenaline flow.

SUNDAY CYCLIST

The Sunday cyclists are not fast riders
Enjoying the warm sun on bare legs
unaware their life is in hands of drivers

Unperturbed, happily peddling slowly along
without wing mirrors they cannot see
the traffic behind forming an angry throng

Older drivers will wait for their moment
but often the young will push their luck
and quickly pass with lack of judgement

The cyclist wearing black, disappears
from sight when entering the shadows
of large overhanging bushes and trees

A touch from a wing-mirror or handle-bars
not noticed by the van or car can flip
the cyclist into the path of following cars

If the rider doesn't go under a car wheel
bare skin on tarmac will be bloody and hurts
and gravel rash takes a very long time to heal

Year 2016.

MUMBAI Haiku

Bombay in 1950
families slept in the street
and now, they still do

Note. Bombay was renamed Mumbai but it did not make much difference to a lot of people.

In 1950 the population of Bombay was 3,088,811
In 2015 the Metro City of Mumbai had a population of approx. 22 Million, In 2021 it is 20,667,556 inhabitants.

MY CARER

I had lost twenty per cent of hearing
I was going deaf, why?
Was it the wife shouting?
or clay pigeon shooting?
I might be simple, but not dumb
I married an accountant
She is good looking and
feeds me better than my mum

When we went to the Building Society
I smiled at the staff, said "goodbye"
Wife would speak, ask questions
push the forms to me to sign,
Not anticipating the implications
One day I decide to purchase
a motorbike, a bargain
Owner said, "Cash, no complications"

continued

To the Bank I rushed, presented my book
requesting eight hundred cash
“Please speak to the manager”
she replied, giving me a funny look
To the manager I was ushered
He asked, “Where’s your wife?”
“Why”? I inquired, “She is your Carer”
I could not believe what I heard!
I exploded with anger, poor bloke
“I am deaf, not daft or had a stroke.”
Then explained, the glass partition
stops me hearing, so I never spoke
I got the cherished motorbike
Also now have an aid to hearing,
“Do the washing up” that I don’t like.

MY THOUGHT

The past, saved to savour
Present, a pleasant flavour
Next must be, just dust.

LITTLE THINGS

Change that old shirt. I will my **darling**
Did you put on clean pants? Yes said **I**
Don't leave everything to me. But I **don't**
Made a drink! You did not ask what I **want**
You let the cat in the house, close the door **to**
Smokey is my favourite animal, please let it **be**
I will improve. **Darling I don't want to be nagged**

Note. This is my idea of a reverse acrostic and please tell my wife that poetry is a mind game that I play when she is busy cleaning the house,

FIFTY-FIVE AND FIT AS A FIDDLE

Helen, the moment I first set eyes on you
was at our house in Runfold, Surrey in 1962
£2,200 was the price of our house, Wilmslow
To afford it we had a lodger in the room below
That was the same as the E type Jaguar's price
he bought one, then another after crashing twice

The Doctor is late, the midwife sighed
The baby is coming, Ann, your mother cried
The midwife shouted, "Get hot water". What capers
Your mother lay on a bed covered in daily papers
then with legs wide-spread," Push" the midwife said.
You looked out, paused, then shot out onto the bed

continued

I thought it would be difficult, very hard to cope
But you slid out as if you were a bar of soap
Then you smiled so sweetly as there you lay
Perhaps pleased to see me, or the light of day
A happy baby, a cheerful child, young and teen
such a lovely, daughter, you have always been.

ABORTION Senryu

It is their bodies
That's why men should not decide
about abortion

MORE GROWTH

Leaders talk about we need 'More Growth'
expansion, more jobs, Union Brothers
But it's all at the expense of others
Politicians call, to expand the economy
more emigration, more workers muscles
Then, borrow more Euros from Brussels

Not everyone can have lots of everything
clean water, oil, rare minerals, food and fishing
These finite resources will and do cause fighting
Population control or disease will take effect
growth, in their terms is not sustainable
because overpopulation makes it unobtainable

RABBIT HABIT

My wife has a lovely habit
Talking, rabbit, rabbit
I wish she would hush
not twitter like a thrush
I need quiet to study, I am a dunce
A man can't do two things at once
I am fond of peace and quiet
but live with sounds of verbal riot
In amongst life's noise and clatter,
and background of my wife's natter
When she calls me, I wonder
can it out do nature's thunder
When at last she is asleep, her snore
will emit even through the door
When I finally join her to sleep
she wakes up to talk, I tend to weep
then she smiles, an angelic smile
Never mind she'll sleep in a while.

DREAMING

I had a nightmare
I dreamt my wife was ugly
I woke up. She is.

Don't tell her about this poem, it's our secret.

PERCEPTION BY PARTICLES

What I think is me and what is you
Is purely a pile of chemicals and water
held together by a mysterious glue

Life is how you imagine it should be
Your reality is not my idea of reality
You choose how it looks, what you see

Views of right or wrong change in time
Your ideas of love will be different to me
Other people's dreams will not mimic mine

Gluons neutrons subatomic particles
Protons hydrogen atoms, electrons
Truly, we are a strange pile of eclectic articles

Note. It is strange that a pile of chemicals and particles somehow become charged with what we call life and can then communicate with other piles of particles. Humans can break down and analyze all the component parts and properties but cannot create life.

THE ENEMY WITHIN

The enemy that will threaten a sovereign state
have already driven past the fortress gate
Their Trojan horse is their Human Rights

For quite a while there will be no riot or fights
living quietly as a community until a given date
Working for the cause while they busily procreate.

FRIENDS OR FIENDS

Often you will find
in life, your wife or husband
is your only one true friend

Senryu

LEADERS THAT LEAD WITH LEAD

Have you seen how genial
genocidal killers can be
They go on public view
for all the world to see
With charming smile
and airbrushed face
Remember they can destroy and
do remove people without a trace
Think about all those leaders, that
were and are without humanity
That can and do cause
killing with equanimity.

THE PERFECT PEARL

Forty years ago, I married the perfect girl
It was like finding, in the immense sea
an oyster that held the perfect pearl
I am so glad that you accepted me
You were just a sapling
and me, already an old tree
May 1980 now seems so far away
The years have passed so quickly
Let's re-marry on our anniversary day.

LANGUAGE Senryu

Chinese Café worker
Irishman ordered breakfast
"Take your Fork-n-knife"

My wife said this to a customer in our café.
Alf's Café at Runfold, on the A31.Farnham, Surrey

LIFE Haiku

Life is a calm sea
Interesting to explore
Full of stinging things

RED WINE WHITE WINE

My wife and I were invited to a function
by The Master of a London Lodge
To join their society was my assumption
We sat at the high table set for fifty
gifts of gold for each lady present
Waiters served each course swiftly

My wife, unaccustomed to British society
sat opposite me, looking elegant
but strangely subdued, sitting quietly
Conversation was light, moving round the table
Waiters served the wine for fish and meat.
Seeing my wife sip the wine, I think she is able

She on this occasion, tried each wine
had always been teetotal. But now
thought it best to try to, wine and dine
Then she decided to speak, her eyes glistened
as she addressed my friend, The Grand Master.
The guests stopped eating, they all listened

"You drink white wine and then the red.
It all goes down the same way
and comes out the same colour", she said
A little polite laughter cut through the ice.
The Lodge never asked me to join? To say
the evening seems a blur, will now suffice

Have I missed anything? I don't think so.
My wife is the most important part of my life
I hope we have many more years to go.

IF Haiku

If you have Cancer
Do you worry about dirt
No, you just worry

A TIGER DEAD

Many years ago toothpaste tubes
were made of lead
Every morning when I clean my teeth
I see toothpaste and a tiger dead
Man and many creatures
lead bullets have killed
But this will never not stop
This image, in my brain was filled

Let me pick up the toothpaste
to remember and tell you
It was television in the fifties
A story of dare and do
The brave naked native, plus film crew
Snarling tiger in his jungle lair
The camera watching closely
What I saw, was not very fair

continued

The penniless poacher placed empty
tubes of toothpaste in a cooking pot
Those harmless charmless, empty tubes
then melted down to liquid, very hot
Ah, those tubes were made of lead
He poured the molten metal into a mould
making bullets for his antique gun
A wonder of ingenuity to behold

Black powder measured carefully
into the long barrel, then the ball
with a bit of his vest, as wadding
Adverts burnt off, but I still recall
Then the chase, hardly, it was a walk
The tiger was squatting in defensive mode
Huge young beautiful male, superb sight
Barely ten feet away, I hear the gun explode

Note. Sadly, all tigers will soon be dead.
I cannot brush my teeth without remembering
It is one of my most memorable but sad poems.

KEEP THE PEACE

Turn away, and don't turn back
To try to understand, puts you on the rack
Ten words are enough to get hurt and to kill
so release yourself in poetry, keep that tongue still.
When getting verbal abuse; be careful what you say
Consider the speaker an empty barrel, they will float away

AN UNFORGETABLE TASTE

Better than eating a chocolate bar
Sweeter than honey, softer than cream
The best taste in the world by far

I know what every mother has done
and what every dad should do
That is, kiss and gently bite their baby's bum

And that sweet smell of new baby
will linger for life in your nose
An odour better than Bisto gravy

My kids are growing sinewy and quite tough
and their hair has little streaks of grey, I still
love to kiss their skin although it's rather rough.

WHITE LIES

Being generous truthful and honest
most often totally and badly backfires
Because people just cannot believe it
then accuse you of being thieves and liars

I tried my best to be truthful and generous
it did not work. That's where the problem lies
No matter how much money or aid is given.
better to avoid the truth, if must, tell white lies

No matter how much food or help is given
because 'YOU CAN', by individuals, or a Nation
Think carefully for it often ends in accusations
of self-interest. Resulting in anger and indignation

SEEING RED OR GREEN WITH ENVY

The traffic light was red
in the town, so there I sat
on my old Triumph triple

A bike came up behind
ticking over prr-at, prr-at
I did not turn to look

I knew it was a Super-size, four
by its roar, ridden by a prat
He was tempting me to race

At a glance, he knew I was old
He revved, brat- brrat, the rat
Look at me, the noisy message said

My clothes are cheap, helmet open face
He would have better gear, spoilt brat
I did not bite, waited for the show

Off he went, at Amber, nearly Green
Megaphones blasting brr-at, brr-at
All of a hundred metres on his Superbike

Then taking his hands of the handlebars
boldly in silver suit, up the brat sat
to adjust his gloves, and preen

For one second, I hoped he'd fall off
but then thought, I've done all that
and being amused, drove slowly home

Year 2014.

DO NOT DIE THIS WAY

One line is enough to say
My friend died on a summer day
Burnt to death in a car, please pray
That loved ones don't go this way

My skydiver friend Ray Etchell, Para regiment was killed in a car crash

A SERENE SCENE

Numerous birds twitter and tweet
proposals to meet high above the ground
Stately pines soar stiffly skywards
as if gravity has been ignored, overcome
Woodpeckers tap, rat-a-tat-tat
on a dead birch tree they have found
The fruit trees climb and spread
ready to catch the short summer sun

Dainty deer dance with boundless bounds
and create a regular drumming sound
The rhododendrons creep and try
to cover others, to smother and overcome
Restless rabbits fertilize the soil
by piling poo pellets in a mound
Then various grasses grow and thrive
where once there was none or some

continued

Oak trees kill all the opposition
with tannins of which acorns abound
Green fronds of fern insidiously spread
where their underground tubers freely run
Foxes looking for cats or household scraps
as they circle constantly round and round
Lily of the valley spread out wide
Giving perfume free to everyone

Voles and moles are rarely seen here
but they are there, tunnelling underground
Narrow tracks and paths appear
where the deer and rabbits run
Deer ticks are carried and transfer
mice to deer, deer to human, round and round
Nettles nicely cover burnt fire ashes
after fly tipping by an unknown bum

Nice grass snakes eat frogs and toads
Adders hide in sweet heather that they found
Beech trees spread wide their canopies
To kill their neighbours daughter and son
While larch and pine cover mosses with acid
from leaves and seed, wind has downed
Red poppies grow above an interred body
above where a dastardly deed was done

AN ARRESTING ADVENTURE

Sailing from Chichester in my yacht Rub-A-Dub-Dub
to visit Nelson's HMS Victory at Portsmouth Harbour hub
over the Chichester sand banks called a bar
sailing with light wind, note, quicker by car
It was a sunny day, with mirror calm sea
Tide coming in, getting deeper, lucky for me
My wife said, "what are those metal posts and beam?"
It was a submerged submarine barrier, I'd never seen

Directly underneath our keel, a barrier, there it was,
there is a gate, but I missed it. Tide carried us across
We entered Portsmouth, past Ark Royal aircraft carrier
The huge ship was home to the jump jet plane, 'Harrier'
I steered by wind and tide in masterly fashion, docked
beside wharf steps, disappointed, nobody had watched
My wife and regulation two kids, did then disembark
on an adventure to explore Victory, what a great lark

As we toured this fantastic ship of English oak
filled with cannons, guns and artefacts. A bloke,
a Royal Marine, was constantly watching me
following wherever we went, very annoyingly
Perhaps he fancies me, I thought, I ignore him
can't he see, I have a wife, nice and slim
As we depart from our extensive, grand tour
walking the plank, down to the concrete shore

continued

I am arrested, by the Sergeant Marine and troop
and escorted to an Officer in his hut, or Cuckoo coop
Why am I under arrest, I ask quite politely
“For coming ashore here, we do not treat that lightly
we might even confiscate you sailing craft
There is a sign. Do not anchor, are you daft?”
A large sign said, NO ANCHORING, “Ah”, I cried
“Sir, I did not anchor, it was with rope I tied.

The sign is also facing inland, may I also say
Seaward side is blank, it should face the other way
“Sir, please leave right now, my men will assist”.
“Thank you, Captain; I will do, as you insist”!
The tide was still running into the harbour
so I used the engine, easier to manoeuvre
Seeing a stepladder in the water, flotsam afloat
a danger to propellers or any speeding boat

I lifted it on board, a good deed, I thought with pride
Then the engine stopped, we drift back with the tide
right under the bow of the Ark Royal, then our mast
jammed, under the upward curving bow, stuck fast.
The Harbour Police launch came to our rescue
Plastic sheet had blocked the water intake, phew
Then, “Oh dear, the policeman said, I see; I see
You have purloined a piece of HMS property”

“Can’t you see that it is wet, saltwater, Sergeant
I simply retrieved it to save a serious accident”!
With stern face, and full of utter disbelief
Transferred the ladder, and to my relief
Said, we will escort you out the harbour, to sea
Don’t come back. You, we do not wish to see
My boat is banned, my seamanship in tatters
The end of a perfect day that is all that matters.

DEAR-OH-DEAR

Dear can sound formal, or sometimes polite
May even be sardonic which just isn't right
A homophone turns it into venison or Bambi
Sometimes just sounds a bit namby-pamby
So let's stick with 'Hi', an excellent choice
One that can be projected with confident voice.

Note. Does anyone say 'namby-pamby' anymore? It seems to have disappeared from popular use. The term was actually coined 280 years ago to ridicule the poetry of Ambrose Philips by his contemporaries Alexander Pope and Henry Carey.

DREAMS

If you work hard, it can and will happen
If you just laze around and think of gloom
You will end up dozing dopily to your doom

TABOO Haiku

It is my firm view
Tattoo's will become taboo
Skirts go up and down!

GUNPOWDER PLOTS AND PLOD

I am proud of my son
how he has carried on
in the face of adversity
I could not have done
the battles that he has won
with the mental anguish of MS

He was a strong-willed child
Politely, he was a little wild
I am glad that it was that way
at the State School, they could not cope
so, I sent him private, much more scope
Cross Country Champ, and Rugby captain

I'd shown him stuff, I learnt in the Army
Then he did something absolutely barmy
Dismantled shotgun shells, for gunpowder trails
Blew up small dams, his ingenuity never fails
Headmaster said, your son is expelled, he is a fool
He set gunpowder trails in corridors of our school

My reply, I was in the Army Royal Engineers
used to use explosive without fears
I taught Bernie to lay a fuse
This is a place of learning, is it not?
He did no damage; it's not a gunpowder plot
He demonstrated knowledge, like you do!

continued

The Master condescended to forget
But young Bernie, was not done yet
He decided to be creative at school.
Diligently working in the school workshop
A steel pipe, drilled a little hole on the top
threaded and closed the end. It was a Cannon

A cannon ball was required, a shotte, or shot
They are quite rare, it's interesting what he got
A metal table leg ball, with bits smoothed off
From the end of the rugby field, with his peers
amongst the thick rhododendron bushes he peers
Aims the five-foot cannon at the spires, and fires

The cordite smoke takes them all by surprize
The shot, over the stately school, it flies
The bang and smoke, gave their position away
After a minor beating, by a Master of the school
and thrown forcefully into the swimming pool
Bernard decided to give more respect, to be cool.

A true account of my son Bernard's adventures at Pierrepont School Frensham, Nr Farnham,, Surrey. Circa 1974.

Note. He became a policeman, a big surprise to me, why? Bernie had many visits by police when he was a teenager, mainly about riding motorbikes that he had built and was hurtling around the countryside on, no tax or insurance did he pay. Until he got snared one day. It was a terrible shock for such a healthy adventurous young man to suffer multiple Sclerosis after being a Police driver and motorcyclist for 15 years.
PIERREPONT SCHOOL was at Frensham, Nr Farnham Surrey.
They did a great job with both of my sons, regrettably it closed.
It is now a centre for religious studies.

DISAPOINTMENT

Anticipation
queued all day to see the Queen
drove past at high speed.

Senryu.

Note. My son was five years of age.

MY PARTNER MY PAL

She lies beside me, asleep and peaceful
The power of her brain at rest
Animal power is so graceful, beautiful

I lay my hand on her skin
and feel the strong beat of
her kind warm heart within

She is her ladyship, I the gardener
I am her guardian, she my child
She is my dresser I her un-dresser

Life has been interesting and so wild
Slow 40s, fast 50s. Tamed in the 80s
I do wish we could have had a child

She is the finest person I have known
during my life of eighty-two years
Others when hard times came, have flown

She is the Queen, I am the Knave
I am the King, she my concubine
She is my master and my slave.

WANDERLUST

Should she stop serenading you by singing sweet silly songs
Or whisper willingness over shared wanton wants and lust
Warmth has waned, with winsome ways, she's gone
wanderlust

Note. This came to mind because of the caring way my wife covers me while I am asleep.

CHAIRS Senryu

Chairs must get stronger
Lawyers are waiting for their break
from those big wobbly bottoms

THE MAN IN BLACK

There was a murmur, a rumble, then a roar
An infernal machine has arrived at my door
With trepidation, I peep, prepare to weep
The man in black has come, perhaps to reap

Black leather, shining helmet, fearsome in this guise
his voice muffled by the mask, bright blue eyes
The machine which carried him, I could tell
was not made in heaven, more likely in hell

continued

Inscribed in dripping letters, rouge et noir
on the tank stated, Terminator or Abattoir
When the brute realized I could not hear
he removed his helmet and also my fear

This was my baby boy, now not so small
wide smile on his face, in his boots 6ft tall
Now on close inspection the words could be seen
it was Dominator in red black and dark green

Come for a ride with me, a trip, a laugh, a jolly
Yes said I, remembering my last ride was a folly **
Setting off this summer day, air warm and dry
past Crooksbury Hill, then Elstead, oh my!

What a pleasant time but so quickly gone
The music of the engine softly purring along
this was the route that my nephew Robert took
this was different, comfortable, I relaxed to look

Thursley Common and Sailors Lane, very steep
I remember this place, my wife fell out of a jeep
Now sitting on the back, with no control, Oh No
it's like a Bucking Bronco, Hips slide to and fro

Sliding down the stony steps, trees all around
broken parts of bikes lay strewn on the ground
Regret to say, I got off, better safe than sorry
rather home on the bike than breakdown lorry

continued

Lovely views, birch and fir, muddy river, slipping, sliding
muscle twitching, smell of hot oil and leather, sun shining
Through woods, over hills, gripping tight, muscles pulling
Over Frensham Common, deep sand, twisting, turning

Here are memories of Pierrepont School, happy days
The rider of this bike was my young son Marc,
who was taught good mannered ways
Up the Bourne Road, past friends in bed still asleep
Tilford and home, great two hours, a memory to keep.

THE LITTLE GREENFLY

A tiny greenfly landed on my windscreen
Translucent wings and long antennae
so tiny, he could hardly be seen

Let us assume it to be a 'He'
Blown away, into his outer space
by a passing car, from his tree

How can such a tiny creature
find a mate, in a world
of trees, ponds and pasture

That would seem infinite to him
a pond, like the Atlantic Ocean
I don't think that he could swim

He can't, chat on a phone
use dating agencies or
organize parties, at his home

continued

Our World seems extremely small
helped by Face-book and phones
and the ability to give a girl a call

Then by car, ship or plane
travel across oceans to court.
this greenfly cannot do the same

He flew off, at the next traffic light
to me a distance of a mile
to him a solar system, like a rocket flight.

MARC TAKE CARE

Marc, you are thirty-nine years old, Wow!
So take care of your money right now
Will he make it to half century?
Old age can be a life in penury

Perhaps I should be quiet, not tell
You cannot silence Father Time's bell
Tick, tock, we can stop those chimes
but that will not stop those ageing lines

Hair starts growing out your spreading nose
the ears get larger, and the big belly grows
The trouble with growing old
it arrives too quickly so I am told

continued

It is a misnomer, The Golden Age
it is false, more like Cold in Age
The benefit of not going to work all week
is muscle ache, bones creak, bladders weak
All T.V. programmes you have seen before
old news, Soaps, adverts, repeats galore
The kids seem to talk a different language
they want to be seen as cool, not average

But being an Old Fart does have benefits
it does not matter if the £5-00 suit fits
And a bed is where you fall asleep and rest
you can wear a Baby-grow or thermal vest

You can be cheeky, almost anything goes
without getting punched on your rosy nose
Finally to compensate for such old age
you can act as if you are clever, A Sage.

PEOPLES PERSON Haiku

President Zuma
A poor man of the people
has bought a Boeing.

EXTERMINATE, EXTERMINATE

At the same time that we are told
there are seven million people in this world
Scientists have a formula, to stop growing old

They have an anti-ageing formula
I see a problem looming for every Ma and Pa
Every child wants food, water, house and car

One child, or accept abortion? Highly implausible
Mile high tower flats, stop using cars, risible
Stop reproduction, more food production, impossible

There is already starvation in Southern Africa
for years the UN has been feeding Somalia
On-going food shortages exist in North Korea

Bangladesh and Bangkok flood, can they manage?
Already there is a housing and clean water shortage
Rising seas will cause much more lasting damage

Humans all have the urge to reproduce, to recreate
we cannot continue at this rate, or the Oldies fate
will be decided by the young crying, EXTERMINATE-
EXTERMINATE.

Note. This was said by the Daleks in the 1966 Science Film
Daleks Invasion of Earth 2150 AD.
I am an Oldie, so you can see my concern.

GIN PALACE Haiku

Only ten yachts at sea
Thousand in the harbour
What are they used for?

Note. I had a yacht, but I sailed it, so you need not answer my question.

LOVE CAN CHANGE

Sex, making babies is called mating
It is not love, it's recreating
Love is separate from sexual pleasures
I will try and explain with different measures

Love can grow, slow, change, or diminish
love can lead to marriage, change and finish
I loved my mother all my life from a child
except when as a teenager, I was wild

I loved the adrenalin of the sexual chase
with the usual urge to increase the human race
I loved the fear of sky-diving, pulsating high
but I certainly did not have a wish to die

I love my sons with a type of love, that's rough
love for my daughter is different, soft, she is tough
Love can diminish, disappear, I've married twice
learn from past errors, mistakes, it will not be thrice

continued

Love must be nurtured, not allowed to freeze
or it will drift away, cool down, fly away on a breeze
Love is not permanent, undying, or has clarity
it must be reflected, worked at, with parity

Love can have different levels, shades, aspects
I love my cat, he responds, talks, it reflects
Love, keeping it and the enemy away, a war
keep some ammunition, stay awake, don't be a bore

Love of my wife is reflected in how she shares
the worries we all meet in life, it shows she cares
I know that this cannot cover matters all
but I must close now, I heard my wife call.

HAVE CARAVAN Senryu

Bought electric car
Three hundred miles on one charge
One -fifty towing

POETIC ATTITUDE

I have atti-chewed
you have atti-tood
Neither can you say nyther
and continue with neether
We duel over shed-uel
you will fight for sked-uel
In lieu of saying Leftenant
you fight for the lootenant
Our garage is english Gaa-raj
yours a french version Garidj
We properly pronounce Toma-toe
You improperly say Tomay-toe
Chips, you have to Frenchy-fy
to an absurd French Fries, why?
The letter Z is not Zee
It is definitely Zed, you see
So Zebra is Zeb-bra
not silly Zee-bra
and Bouy is pronounced Boy
not Boo-ee, it's more like ahoy
Nuclear cannot be Nukil-ar
it's New-clear, is that clear
Iraq, irritably spoken as Eye-rak
is irrefutably in English, I-rack
I am not adverse to say Vayze
for there is not an R in Vase
No need for risible ree-search
I agree to differ, after my research.

I wrote this to send to my poet friend Aesthete2000 in America.

BEING OLD Haiku

A fresh coat of paint
why? The house is warm and dry
and soon I shall die!

BOB ACRAMAN

Robert was an educated, gentle gentile child
Only his family thought he was quiet, mild
But others knew he was precocious, wild
Entered the Army Parachute Regiment
Really that's not what his parents meant
They wanted a civilian, he would not relent

Athletic, army trampoline champ, a trier
Corporal in rank, he wanted to get higher
Reacted to RSM's abuse consequences dire
Actually lost his stripes to his superior's grief
Mangled RSM's finger with his set of teeth
And started Skydiving, much to his relief
Nigeria his home now, a General my belief.

Note. The part of the above poem about the RSM was when he was a corporal and the RSM wagged his finger at Bob's face while lecturing him on being untidy. Bob bit the RSM's finger so he lost his stripes. Robert was an extraordinary Skydiver it was most probably due to him being excellent on the trampoline before starting skydiving.
I wrote this as an acrostic poem where the first letters spell out his name.
He emigrated to Nigeria became a General, then opened a night club. But died out there about about 20yrs ago.

DEAR-OH-DEAR

Dear can sound formal, or sometimes polite
may even be sardonic which just isn't right
A homophone turns it into venison or Bambi
Sometimes just sounds a bit namby-pamby
So let's stick with 'Hi', an excellent choice
One that can be projected with confident voice.

Note. Does anyone say 'namby-pamby' anymore? It seems to have disappeared from popular use. The term was actually coined 280 years ago to ridicule the poetry of Ambrose Philips by his contemporaries Alexander Pope and Henry Carey.

THE PLACID SEA

Under the surface of that calm placid sea
Seemingly a safe place for you and me
All creatures live in fear of being another's meal
It's not a safe place on the sunny surface
for a soft skinned person of the human race
to sharks looking up, they think you are a seal

Below there are long translucent stinging strings
Squid with sharp beaks and other clingy things
also torpedo shaped killers with toothy jaws
Others lay very still and quiet and wait
like the Angler fish with wiggly worm bait
and Stonefish that suck victims into maws

continued

Even the gentle whales you might go to see
wallowing on vacation in the Southern sea
kill and eat squid, krill and lots of little fish
Doggone it, only the Dugong or Manatee
it seems will not eat or harm you or me
but crabs find our dead a very tasty dish.

THE SEA Haiku

Most desirable
lovely seaside beachside view
killer when incensed.

PROSPERITY

Private, policed, protected palisades of
portentous palaces with pillared porticoes where
motionless magnificent Mercedes motors make the
picture perfect polished perception of prosperity.

Servants silently slave serving superb servings of
delightful, decorative delicious dishes designed to
tastefully tempt to tickle tastebuds totally, till
falling faint feeling full, fasting followed until

The masseuse massages, manipulating muscles.
Painfully pressing pressure points persistently
teasingly tortured till tiny tears trickle, "TONG",
I cry. (Pain) Klang, an area of Kuala-Lumpur, Malaysia.

THE ENGLISH DAME

The English Dame, when out on the street
of Badshot Lea, decided to eat brunch
of potato inkhorn and egg instead of lunch
With a loaf of bread and glass of mead
She mused; she was in debt no money
but had chattels; there-fore no need to worry
A Scot came by. in his local dialect said
"Hello" gis a kiss for tea." She replied but wasn't rude
take away your merry riddle, wicked wee dude"
Then he, lifting his plaid kilt, said
"What an unfriend, Ok Bye y 'all"
Showed her his doobry and arse, what gall.

By Simpleton on Dec 24, 2011. © Bernard Green

I am proud of this little poem as it was my entry for the prestigious David Crystal poetry competition in the Daily Telegraph. On the 06/12/2011.

I was advised that I was on the short list of fourteen entries and my poem was be published in the Daily Telegraph.
The poem had to be no more than 100 words using at least 25 words from David Crystal's list of English words.

A NEW VENICE Senryu

People are building on the sand
Global warming, the sea will rise
creating a new Venice in Florida

LIFE Haiku

Life is a clean river
Inviting you for a swim
Full of piranha

LOVING AND MARRIAGE

It trips off the tongue too easily, often
Love is such an easy word to say
It's used to describe many things
Love my car, have a lovely day

We show love in many different ways
loving our family, horse, dog, or cat
And when blessed with children
we love them lots, we all know that

When first you meet, it's all visual
chemistry, pheromones and genes
Later you will enjoy your spouse
in other ways and different means

Love can be of many types and shades
It will be varied powerful and strong
like Jacob's coat that he wore
Sometimes sweet as a skylark's song

Love can be confusing, for with love
anger can be close at hand
Marriage can bond you tight together
with meeting of the minds, it's grand

continued

The passion of a lasting clinging kiss
can be replaced by a silent look
Which will be understood by you
and the meaning could fill a book

This world is meant to be chaotic
stress and upset is the norm
to test your strength and your will
Together you can find peace and form

Marriage, an act, so strong a deed
and sanctified by the Lord above
We gather in the house of God to
share this, the highest bond of love

We gather here to witness marriage
not in fear and trepidation.
The next hymn, Jesus loves you
Sung with feeling, love and elation

Here we have love in its finest way
Two persons on this stage, in an act
with faith in one another, to marry
and prove it in front of all, in fact

Your life will not run straight and true
like a bullet or Channel Tunnel train
it'll twist and turn with ups and downs
but order will come in your domain

continued

Then you will laugh, not cry when you
find the moth has eaten your woolly hat
You will giggle and share the joke
and say, “I hope he enjoyed eating that,

When your wife sets out your tasks
those jobs to do when she is going out
Be content, when it was woman’s work
to do the dishes, machines were not about

And when your dear wife’s snoring
keeps you wide awake all the night
think not of waking her, but listen
and to its music, think of words to write

WINTER WOOLIES

The Nepalese arrived from overseas
as the leaves were shed from the trees
Without suitable warm thick winter clothes
their slim bodies froze from nose to toes

New was too expensive, they all concurred
So they walked for miles quite undeterred
Far and wide across countryside, to Car Boots
in pursuit of coats, hats suits and furry boots

Their colourful appearance in apparel of Nepal
will submerge slowly, until they are not seen at all
Note. The Gurkha soldiers were based in Aldershot, Hants,
for many years now many families live there.

NAGGING

If you think your wife is always nagging
or seems to be
and your love for her is flagging

Before you walk out the door
Consider this!
you might not have been loved before

Parents might have been too busy working hard
to put food on the table
while you were playing in the yard

Now the loving wife worries about your health
and your well-being!
Worrying about you, not your wealth

So think carefully about the words she uses
What is it all about
Your beer belly, smoking or other abuses

Are you doing things like helping in the house
or saying that that's the women's job
Pretending you are tired and acting like a louse

You had better ask yourself, is she right
don't make excuses
Mine is unfortunately. Oh, always be polite

MY SUN Senryu

Life without my Peg
Would be like life without the sun
Quite impossible

LIFE INSURANCE Senryu

If you are thinking
of having Life Insurance
Don't pay, it will stop

IMMIGRATION Haiku

People in poverty
due to global warming
Which way? North is best

Note. Desert sands are expanding.

HOT AND COLD (Adult poem)

Have you ever chased
a naked lissom lady
through deep pristine snow
and felt hot blood course
your body in a burning glow
We climbed the mountain
across snow with icy crust
It was a sunny winter day
We were on a slippery slope
both with an intent to play

I chose a very peaceful spot
She was hot, snow so cold
We were not too young or old
Was it love? Perhaps just lust
I will just let the story unfold
We were both bare, without a care
She lay beneath me, loving me?
On the deep icy cold snow
She did not complain or cry
I never asked, I will never know

For every action, there is a reaction
and here was no exception
As we started to play
With arms outstretched she slid
off downhill, very quickly away
She looked like a shooting star
as she cried out, Au revoir
Where she went, nobody knows
Leaving me with just a memory
and a bag of her 1960s clothes.

PROTECTING PLOD 05/04/2013

To avoid a Police Health and Safety insurance claim
When burglars burgle your business or home
If you have to call the Plod, make it your aim
If you let the police enter you establishment
be it freehold or a leasehold property
It seems you must first make a full risk assessment
Before Plod enters make sure you mop the floor
of any blood, bodily fluids or grease or water for
If they slip, the lawyers will certainly make you poor
After your window or door was broken in the raid
Collect the glass and cover it or any scratch will ensure
you will be bankrupt after police compensation is paid
Then the next Insurance premium will be raised
While the criminals are rarely found or punished
The police will get gongs and officers highly praised.

Note. A policewoman sued the owners of a garage because she tripped over something in the darkness.
She should have had a torch, don't you think.

HUMOUR (Adult poem)

I was told that in far off Kazakhstan
there were three women to every man

So I thought I'd take a holiday there
and see if there was any going spare

continued

Then I was told that some are not such nice ladies
Catch you, by getting pregnant for maintenance fees

I've seen on late TV, naked ladies of different races
holding phones and pulling the most peculiar faces?

So I decided to keep my money in the bank
watch the television and have a walk.

Note. This is mainly manly fun and mickey taking.
A friend of mine was working in far off Kazakhstan

CONTENTMENT

When I was a child
I desired to be older
When in peaceful valleys
I wanted to be on the hills

When on Terra Firma
I longed for the heaving sea
When caught in tumultuous ocean
I prayed for church and quiet devotion

When in sticky steamy Jungle
I wished to be in temperate lands
When obliged to drive slowly
I itched to drive faster

When watching birds
I envied their wings
When flying hot Hot-Air balloons
I completely forgot all those things.

INTERNET DATING

There both hunting
they are looking on the web
each with their reasons

I look for a man
A handsome man with a job
One that I can love

I look for a girl
that I can make a victim
I pretend I'm rich

PISA HISTORY Haiku

Tower of Pisa
Obscuration, procrastination
Equals pile of rubble.

A WAIL

Befriend a whale
The Japanese will thank you
Easier to harpoon.

The Japanese are killing whales. Why? It's profit. They pretend it is for research but plenty of whales are dying on the beaches probably due to military sonar type noises. They could all be examined. They are probably making pet food, getting oils and making perfume from ambergris.

INFORMATION

All Leaders, past, present, new and old
having gained control of a country's wealth
ensure their pockets are lined with gold

Misinformation is the key
fed by television and radio
to the likes of you and me

Hitler mastered films, for propaganda
combined with radio transmissions
everyone suffered from his megalomania

T.V. and radio then came into play
like scenes from Orwell's, "Nineteen eighty-four"
now it seems to have had its day.

Note. George Orwell's story 1984 is with us now.

MUTATIONS

People are born with mutations
Like me, who is dyslexic
If we all had the same brain
and learnt everything by rote
We would be all doing the same thing
doing the same things. That would be boring
Well, I suppose a lot of people still do
It is the difference that makes things exciting!

I KILLED A SPIDER

A spider came into my view, my vision
as I watched the news on television
I clapped my hands without thinking
and killed this harmless little thing

Then I thought, I should have stopped
taken him to the window and dropped
Then he would have sailed away
on a thread to live another day

I then watched another spin his web
who put the knowledge in his head?
How to spin, to cast adrift on a thread
Is it in the genes, taught or inbred

Tigers, Gorillas, Rhino's I wish to preserve
but spiders, also have a right and deserve
to live, and as they catch irritating flies
which help to improve and protect our lives.

PETROL BOMBS Senryu

Why do police seem
to tolerate petrol bombs
They can kill people.

THE POT OF GOLD

On the fifth January 1994
With my friend Geoff Boyes
Flying a Hot Air Balloon together
In sunny but showery weather
I burn gas, phsst-phsst, and climb
The sun behind us begins to shine

Cumulous clouds around us
Rain made the hot balloon heavy
A dark balloon in front of us did show
It's our shadow surrounded, and aglow
by a complete circular bright rainbow
shining on the puffy white cloud below.

I always wanted to be in the sky
Now you might wonder why
As a child I was often told
There was a pot of gold
At the end of the rainbow
How I found it, I'll tell you so

You already have it, it is life
Although often you will suffer strife

The pot of gold is with you and me
The ability to feel, walk, talk and see
To be able to think and just to be
It is the gift of life, given to us for free

Note. The image of my balloon on the cloud in front of us with a complete circular very bright rainbow in a ring around our shadow was a most beautiful sight and I think is rarely seen

TIME

Sitting in school, time stood still
Eight hours of boring work my fill
Time always drags in a queue
There are times, time flies for you
You are driving a car, half awake
You see an accident, you brake
Time slows, when your life to preserve
Seeing vehicle positions, people to observe
Their faces, their places, the cause the cat
Crunch, slow motion impact, things like that
Time is governed by our brains reaction
While it works out a defensive action.

ALICE IRENE GREEN

Me mum bore me then saw me
I did not awake and cry, so I was
discarded to the rubbish corner
She heard me cry when my head hit
the cold tiled hospital theatre floor
She saved me. Cradled me, fed me
Taught me and fought for me
Nursed me in cold old rooms
through chicken pox and measles
Took beatings till a lover came her way
and disappeared to Scotland for a year

continued

On her return I was twelve or more
I swore at her like a man, rather daring
for I had seen her knock out a man
She slammed me on the floor, sat on me
"I will teach you not to have a filthy mouth"
I loved my mum all my life, I sat beside her
in the hospital, she was aged eighty aged 86
Amazing, after being sold into service at age of 12
then had Tuberculosis when aged sixteen
She said, "Rub my back it's a bit sore." Tired
of sitting in the Cambridge Military Hospital,
she had only been there two days.

A shaft of sunlight shing on her head.
She shook, then her head went back
She was clearly, very quickly very dead
The doctor at the end of the ward
Started to run, to give her aid. I said,
"Don't hurry, don't worry doctor
she has gone up the sunbeam
I know that she is dead."
He looked at me with quiet concern
Not comprehending my feeling or lack
No tears, he could not understand
She had a good long life and departed
up Gods stairway, on a beam of light.

ALICE IRENE GREEN nee SAUNDERS-WHITE

1935

The bonny baby is me!

ME MUM

Me Mum was the one
That paddled my bum
When I lied or was naughty
She was warm, never haughty

The only one that I could trust
Share secrets with, cuddled to her bust
Tucked me into a nice warm bed
Comforted me when tears were shed

After I called my sister a bloody cow
put a bar of soap in my mouth, wow.
Taught me, always to be courteous
even if people are not kind or virtuous

In later life, she and me, most pleasantly
spent many hours chatting, over cups of tea
She never left me. She is there in my genes
In my mind, and sometimes in happy dreams.

Note. My mother had a gentle disposition but with five children, a war on and a husband that was difficult and fond of being aggravating, it was little wonder she occasionally lost her temper.
She developed a strong body from hard work but had a deceiving demure look. When I was about ten years old I saw a man called Leslie Gathergood come in dad's ALF's café, he lived in the village of Runfold and drove a lorry. For some reason he stuck out his strong jaw and invited my mother to punch him, she did but not on his chin but in his solar plexus and laid him out cold.

WOMENS RIGHTS Senryu

Women are equal
Where their rights are restricted
Please do not give aid

POWER Haiku

If I have a gun
I can rule everyone
Unless they have bombs

TO SAVE OR NOT TO SAVE

Many high priests of the past
had false ideas that didn't last
Men that controlled the economy
in their minds was, I, myself-me
Past priests were also politicians
they liked to behave like magicians

Today's monetary priests, like Merkel
are running in a never ending circle
A circle of inflation and deflation
which is no good for any nation
printing money has happened many times before
Countries printing paper money to go to war

continued

Printing paper money is just a business franchise
Banks printing it to increase their power and size
Printing paper money is only a way to create
additional income to fund the Nation or The State
When governments create paper money injections
it causes financial problems, economic distortions

The public think money can be valued by indices
Governments use it to manage money by guesses
Paper currency is absolutely State controlled
Soon you'll find, you are not allowed to own gold
Central banks are buying things that are an asset
Then pay you with paper money while the ink is wet

Governments control money supply by intervention
It started in 12th Cent China. It's not a new invention
History shows it many faults and will create defaults
without the government holding gold in its vaults

When it all ends in tears and disastrous position
The politicians will of course blame the opposition
To spend or not to spend. That is the question.

MOTORBIKE Haiku

An old motorbike
is a man's best possession
or his enemy

HAPPINESS

Material things do not guarantee happiness
Contentment does not depend on what you possess
Money can bring you food, wine and warmth
but not a lovers care in sickness and in health

Don't think that joy is in promiscuity, alcohol or drugs
That is the underworld of thugs and brainless mugs
Happiness is in seeing seeds that you did sow
To have children and see them learn and grow

Freedom to think without outside undue pressure
Having a mind that is kind, has value beyond measure
The ability to enjoy fresh water and the salty sea
and to be able just to walk, talk and feel free.

Authors Note. I have dipped in the dark depths of depravity and have seen the problems that can and will emerge.

MEE-JING, TILLS RING

Flavour enhancer
or MSG flavouring
gives headaches

Haiku poem. Monosodium Glutamate or Mee-jing is what the Chinese call it.

MESSERSMITTS

Swanage town centre
Seagulls dive-bombed people
eating fish-n-chips

Senryu

SOMETHING WRONG? Haiku

Wife and I on train
just I was offered a seat
She does look nurse-like

GIVING GIFTS

When you see someone giving away
lots of money in goods or cash
Consider what's in it for them
and find out if the giver is rash

For most people particularly politicians
freely give away what is not theirs
Gift Aid and other funding abroad
will cost you, your kids and their heirs

If it's lottery money or personal assets
or in a good cause, I do not care
Politicians are giving and spending
your earnings as if it was theirs to share

continued

The Government is splashing cash
abroad in bundles far and wide
Money which costs just paper and ink to print
and will create a rich and poor divide.

Note. The British government has given millions to a private steel enterprise in India, which will be invested in mineral assets. This will increase in value while your printed money will diminish in value like the German Deutschmark did and the Greek Drachma.
Note. In 1951 on the Greek island of Rhodes I paid 10,000 Drachma for a small cup of coffee, I expect you will be doing something similar soon.

OLD AGE Three Hailu's

I can't eat onion's
I'll tell you about my illness
You know I am old.

I carry a phone
Talk a lot about Facebook
I Twitter, I'm young

They write, they line-dance
Tease and please, compose poetry
They are young at heart

BILL THE BAKER 1944 Bill Wilkinson

Bill was a big strong man that
lived in a village called Badshot Lea,
Cottage of hand-made bricks, oak cruck beams
This was where he owned a bakery.

His huge mixing bowl held a sack of flour,
Flour sacks weighed 220 lbs or more
I believe he was stronger than the Black-Smith,
He had to carry the sacks of flour to the upstairs floor.

To keep the dough warm to help it rise,
there was a wooden proving bin, to keep it in.
The loaves were placed in the oven with a long oar like pole,
sandwich bread was turned over in a tin

The wood fired oven, 2ft high 15ft long 10ft wide
built of beautifully built brick arches
In the evening, baking done, he filled the oven with faggots,
Silver Birch swishy branches.

In the morning with a bit of paper he lit those sticks
now being very dry it burnt with ferocious heat.
Then with a mop he cleaned the floor of ash,
Scones cook first, then bread, cakes as it cooled, neat!

The bread tins went in upside down
this put flecks of ash in the crust, it tasted rather nice
The proved loaf was turned over onto the paddle then slid
onto the bricks, a sprig of holly added spice

continued

I collected twelve loaves for Dads Café balanced on my bike
and chewed the crusts while balanced on the handlebars
and brakes,.
I wonder if customers thought mice had been nibbling the bread.
It was a better taste than cornflakes

One day while watching Bill mix the dough
Stripped to the waist, bent over the bin
sweat running from all over his body
and dripping from his arms and chin

I was only eleven years of age, but I said,
"Bill your sweat is going in the dough,"
He laughed, but didn't bother to wipe his brow
"Yes, it is salt; it makes for a better taste you know."

Note. The oven has been demolished but the house is still there. Faggots were bundles of birch tree branches. Many years ago yard brooms were made of those swishy branches.

MARRIED LOVE Senryu

Love and compassion
Necessities, not luxuries
Without them, love dies

FINITE WORLD

How many people can you fit in a phone box
How many can you cram into a car
How many can you pile up in to the sky

How many sheep can you keep in an acre
How many heifers can you feed from hectare
How many people can be fed on hundred hectares

Now think, you are living in a finite space
People will not shrink but they can starve
and the population is exploding rapidly,

Note Global Warming will also reduce the
world food production.

EBOLA'S REACH

With Ebola effectively hiding for twenty-one days
It will be able to catch you in many ways
Closely packed people in a club, a cut or fighting
will be welcomed by this virus that likes bleeding
Shaking hands might end up as a curse
A nod might have to do, that can't get worse

The French have always kissed the cheek
This virus can enter shaving cuts, kill the weak
It might be wise not to have unprotected sex
And don't kiss your cat, it can pass from pets
People that chop and carry wood, cut their meat
A scratch can mean their maker they might meet

continued

Is it on public transport. If it is you cannot tell
A cough or helping hand can mean a road to hell
The cockroaches survived the Dinosaur Extinction
Perhaps half our species might have that distinction.

Note. Those that wish to cross countries borders undetected could be ill, leaving the population unprotected.

MARS

Mars, yes, we all know it is there
and quite frankly I do not care
if it is very hot or horribly cold
or there is water or lots of gold

Here on earth, stars twinkling in the night
are obscured by a smog of scattered light
from street-lamps always burning bright
I do not think that this is right

During this economic recession
why not learn such a simple lesson
and save electric consumption, plan it
Fit time switches, to help our planet

A rocket has just gone off to Mars
yet our children cannot see the stars
Mars is over nine months travel away
better to spend the money here, I say

continued

Over one million youngsters out of work
mostly those that do not wish to shirk
The cost of just one exploratory rocket
would help many with an empty pocket

Does it all make sense to any of you
does it have any commercial value?
Why give all that finance and respect
There must be a hidden military aspect.

THE FLAT

Who's knocking the door
I don't know. Where's the back door
Sorry, there isn't one

Haiku. **Note.** Young and dangerous days

DARK NIGHT Senryu

A quiet dark night
the sentry silently smokes
Bullet stubs his life.

STEVE THE CLIMBER

Steve is from Wales, has lots of tales
Enjoys the company of a pretty female
Runs up high hills and down the dales
Of Irish descent, lean and mean no fat at all
A tree climber, lumberjack, artist, woodcarver
Risks his life for hardly any reward at all

Excellent vocabulary, has nice turn of phrase
A hard worker, untidy, needs a woman
Lives in a caravan, very cold on winter days
Six feet tall, sharp features, reads a lot,
Money avoids him, so he does not gamble
Have not seen him drink alcohol or take pot

When at the top of tall trees
like a sailor atop the high mast
He sways around in the breeze
He has fallen more than twice
Saved by his ropes and skill
Daily danger for low pay; Not nice.

Steven Faherty is also an artist and wonderful wood carver. He was kind enough to paint the cover for my book 'Building the Khufu Pyramid-Shedding New Light on the subject'.

HOW OLD PEOPLE DISAPEAR

have you noticed how the
old people tend to disappear
The young do not listen to you
"You're talking history" they jeer
More so if you are going deaf
and cannot hear the 'Upper Clef'

Young children will only address you once
with no reply, they regard you as a dunce
What they do not realize, although not nice
is that history repeats it's self twice or thrice
The old have seen it happen all before
seeing the young in error makes them sore

Words and music always change with time
Youth tend to copy others, and toe the line
I as an oldie I think that Rap is awful crap
When young I thought ill of Ballet and Tap
If you have a large yacht and Lamborghini's
muscular men will abound and girls in bikinis

TRAFFIC CONES

Are you puzzled and annoyed by traffic cones
that line the roads for mile on mile
Like alien self-generating gnomes
And the police do not get involved or care
Why they are there everywhere stopping traffic,
leaving highways empty, bare

continued

At the end of three of miles or so
there will be a solitary grass-cutter
On a wide verge wearing bright day-glow
Why are there so many of those cones?
Because each one is charged by the hour
making money, so deaf to all your moans

Note. Health and Safety is used as an excuse.

CAR DREAMS

Car adverts, will always show,
as if you will be on your own
Promising freedom to roam
Join the select club, be the one
be part of the elitist throng
comfort, speed. How very wrong

Join the traffic jam, the long queue
No toilets for more than twenty miles
Need a pee, and sitting on aching piles
Fuming at the many miles of cones
one lane open, on the motorway
As two men are cutting the grass today

Your new sporty car is hard
to keep below that speedo red line
You pay the taxes, the tolls, and the fine
You'll need lots of cash at the Motorway Cafe
A must, do not fall asleep, "Have a break"
expensive food and coffee, to stay awake

continued

Adverts do not show, watching for cameras
Police bikes, radar traps, vans, unmarked car
You must though, or you will not get very far
I know you want to be Greener, Carbon Aware
But trains are not cheaper, and getting dearer
so you are forced by circumstance to keep her.

Note. Governments lied about the benefits of diesel to increase their tax revenue. Oil prices went down drastically but petrol pump prices don't.

NEPALESE NURSES

Fill our hospitals
So would our hospital work?
If they were not there

DYSLEXIC

She wrote that I was clever
nobody has ever called me
that in all my life. No not ever
It helps me with my self-esteem
although not sure why it was
said, perhaps it was just a dream

Being dyslexic, I skipped out of school
tired of teachers violence and sneers
Without diplomas, joined life's septic pool
After Merchant Navy, joined the Air Force
but after regarded as a hopeless case
being discharged was my only recourse

continued

Then three years as a Royal Engineer
helped to really change my life
learning without punishment or fear
I have changed my occupation
roughly every ten years, and
enjoyed life beyond expectation

In a life of meeting opinionated Clowns
that despised my lack of schooling
Many fights, lots of ups and downs
He said, " Only those that are intellectual
should live in this village, you should leave".
his pathetic plea to me was ineffectual

Three lovely children, two good wives
First twelve years, second one forever
Chauvinist pig, then a New-man. Two lives
two Café's, Skydiving Centre, Stone quarry
Two planes, 5x Hot Air balloons, all past now
Lot of good times, some trouble, I'm not sorry

It was the American poet Aesthete2000 that surprised me by calling me clever. and encouraged me to write a book.
She did me the honour of writing a description for the back cover of my first book
My first book was called 'Dunce or Dyslexic' and I called myself Simpleton.

BLIGHTON LANE, THE SANDS

Walking in Blighton Lane, Sands, under a sunny sky
as a child of ten in nineteen forty four
I watched a Shire horse and cart come by
with workers sitting on top of hay piled up high
on the wooden four wheeled cart
Only to be losing it on the hedges, why?
After all the effort to cut and load
it was catching on the hedges, either side
because it was only an eigh- foot wide road

I long for the 'Good Old Days.' Do not laugh
Now it's dangerous to walk and enjoy the scene
ride horses or cycle, for there is no path
Cars and vans speed through here every day
on their way to work and back
not realizing it is part of the South Downs Way.

Note. Later than 1945 Horses and Shire horses in Farnham and Guildford were still ploughing the fields, pulling farmers carts and making deliveries of coal, milk, and beer to the houses and pubs. About this time, I was watching a pair of Shire horses raking a field at Runfold. The driver picked up the large metal rake to clear the weeds but dropped it with a crash. One of the horses kicked and caught him in the face. Then both horses broke away and ran up the A31. The last I saw was this poor man with half his face smashed flat, running after them. That was devotion to those horses under his care. I have no idea whether he survived.

THE BLUE RINSE BRIGADE

I was in a strange town, I needed a drink
and was looking for a café
The town was not strange, I was; I think
In there mate, a man said to me
I looked through the door
desperate for a nice cup of tea
I would not go in there, I did say
unless I was blind or dead
It's full of wrinklies, blue rinse and grey
Note. I was only seventy-eight

THE HURCULES

I played leapfrog with the cumulus clouds
High above the noisy cars and crowds
in my big red and blue balloon
but my fun came to an end too soon

When hidden in the likes of a Scottish mist
an RAF Hercules C130 we just missed
On hearing the four engines coming our way
Howard my co-pilot said, " Go down, and pray"

I said we'd better go up in this thick mist
he might go down to drop parachutists
Time seemed to slow down, go slow
as the plane passed a few feet below

continued

The four propellers seemed to be slowly turning
the mist into spiral clouds, slowly churning
The co-pilot looked up at me,
aghast at what he could see!

A bloody great red and blue balloon
Luckily he will be able to report it soon
So close, I could see holding a map
We nearly ended in his lap

Just a few feet, those very few feet
and the Hercules we would meet
and wrap it, a coloured death parcel
We missed, so this story I could tell.

Note, This was in the 1990's over Hankley Common in Surrey. The Army Parachute dropping zone

THE BIG 4x4

It is a big four x four
she'd never driven one before
It is her husband's car
they never travel very far
Never been off the road
in four-wheel drive mode

Hogs the middle of the highway
Lights are on. 'Get out my way'
Thinks she is impregnable
always a metre from the kerb,
It's on a system of yearly hire
so must not scratch as costs are dire

THE JAY Haiku

Piratical Jay
Struts away from the bird's nest
Two songbirds are dead

WHY AM I HERE

Why am I here? This question puzzled me
Luckily, there is so much to do and see
It made me forget about the question
which is a pre-occupation of religion

I have enjoyed most of my long life
despite times of hardship and strife
While I am here, I try to bring cheer
to those around me and that are near

It appears that we need some stress
to keep us straight, out of a mess
The trouble with 'Man' he thinks he's superior
species, when too many become a pest, inferior

Nothing will ever explain why we are here
so as you'll never know, relax; have no fear.

Note. The further you look into space the more the more you should realize how insignificant we are. And how lucky you are to be able to think, see, feel, communicate and share your experiences with your fellow living creatures.

HUMANITY

When a soldier decides to lay down his life
in a thoughtful decision he alone did make
He laid down his life, he was so brave and kind
Medals are then given to remind mankind

When your dog has lost the use
of its hind legs, with ageing
and pleads silently with its eyes
Vets humanely put it down, to be kind

When a racehorse breaks a leg
financial decisions often apply
and humans will then often say
Best we put it down, to be kind

Murderers are given a lethal cocktail
to ensure a painless drift off to sleep
The law says they deserve a humane death
The law often behaves like an ass, I find

When a human is suffering lock-in syndrome acute pain or paralysed and pleads to die, understanding the anxiety of the close family around. Supposedly humane humans say "Oh, No." They are stupid and blind.

Note. Tony Nicklinson a UK resident suffered from Lock-in syndrome. He went to the high court to ask to die humanely. It was refused. A few days later he died with a broken heart and after refusing to eat or drink. Is that humane? His last words were, "Goodbye world, I have had some fun."
I had a friend that asked my advice on suicide. I persuaded him not to do it. Ten days later he collapsed with lock-in syndrome and suffered a long slow mentally painful death. I know because he communicated with me with his eyelids.

POLLUTION

Every bit saved helps
Reduce our carbon footprint
Don't fly fruit and veg

Note. Haiku, the first two lines were in a supermarket advert. Have you noticed the amount of fruit and veg being flown from as far afield as South America.

GROWTH WILL KILL

Politicians advocate growth and production
Too much will mean the end of every nation
The growth explosion of the human species
Means that humans will empty all the seas

The Japanese will consume all types of whales
When tuna which is already in short supply fails
Sharks are going for shark-fin soup by Chinese
when they're gone they will eat anything in the sea's

Easter Islanders outgrew their finite space
Empty Sea's will mean the end of the human race
Look at the recent history if you don't believe me
Africa's Lake Victoria and shrinking Aral-sea

People have started moving for a better life
Overpopulation causes anger and strife
Barriers will get higher and harder to climb
The poor will starve while the mega-rich buy time

continued

That is why those big yachts you see are bomb proof
to sail away in from the common masses, remain aloof
Avoid the populance, fish and hide in the oceans
and avoid the potential rockets and nuclear explosion

Written 19/05/2017.

DAISIES

Daisies open their petals to welcome the sun
to use photosynthesis and be photogenic
Pleasing to see for bug, bee, you, me, everyone

Then they turn their heads to follow the light
until the sunset, when their life-light dims
then to close their petals for the night

The random patterns they create of white
against the background of green-green grass
with yellow spots is truly a delightful sight.

PERHAPS

Perhaps, it was all meant to be, for me
perhaps, too much salt
showed me how to live, you see.

As a child, being the eldest boy
I was used for parenting practice
First being the parents training toy

continued

Not knowing what to do with me
they became terribly frustrated
smacking does not help you see

Unfortunately for them and me
I wet the bed. I tied my winkle
with string, It didn't stop the pee

Perhaps, my father was a masochist
He enjoyed teaching discipline
it was not drink; never saw him pissed

Come back now and you'll get one, or six
if you run away. My dad meant whacks
I had to select the appropriate swishy sticks

World War 2 made things very hard
German planes overflew, bombs boomed
I got whipped if I didn't clean the yard

Perhaps as they didn't know dyslexia was at play
teachers often whipped and punched me
I disappeared, staying away all day

Perhaps I was a chauvinist, Marriage did not last
Three lovely kids though, boy, girl, boy
Re-invented myself and deleted all my past.

LIVING Senryu

Life or existence
I want to enjoy this life
not just to exist.

Year 2015

GIVE AND YOU WILL RECEIVE

If someone gives, with a motive in mind
they will grow bitter and twisted, un-kind
Giving gives me genuine warmth within
does not have to be restricted to kith and kin

A child's twinkling eyes, a smile of joy
is sufficient when you give a toy
Birds freely give voice with song and call
the human listener feeds them in the fall

It is true, give and thou will receive
unless it was in preparation to deceive
I have not read the Bible right through
but what I now believe, may be true

It's the meek, not the brigands band
that will inherit this, our lovely land
I always wanted to see African folk and fauna
but could not bear to witness people's trauma

I remember Bible reading as a child
thinking of meek, being weak, mild
But now I realize it means in interpretation
not about strength, but mild, with education

A SMART COOKIE Senryu

She is a smart cookie
Head for figures, does accounts
Her name is Peggy

My wife.

HER ABSENCE

The silence is not
altered by the television

The coldness is not warmed
by hot drinks or heat.

26/11/2013

Note. My wife was in hospital.

HAVE A NEW WIFE Senryu

I have a new wife
We have a new lease of life
She survived cancer

SEEKING PERFECTION

Life is never perfect
as there always will be strife
Mine is perfect right now, all due to my wife
In all walks of life and business
there will always be Ups and Downs
People can't be perfect, you will always meet clowns

We have lost lots of money, due to dodgy people
but I am content and do not have regrets
As at the moment we do not have any debts
I believe there is a Creator of the Universe
and feel Christian but never go to Church
I'm a Zen Buddhist; don't leave people in the lurch

continued

I was so lucky to have been born in England
in between the World Wars, so sad
to see Wars started with so little cause
We are so fortunate to live in this blessed country
Small Great Britain; protected by the Gulf Stream
such a pleasant place, so fertile, so very green.

THE PERFECT MARRIAGE

There is no such thing
as a perfect partner
But a perfect marriage
is achieved gradually
by each imperfect person
Accepting the others faults
and the imperfections
while enjoying their short
time on this earth with all
its trials and tribulations

IDEAS OF HEAVEN

Eight people arrived at the pearly gate
they were from varied countries or state
They were asked to choose partner or a mate
then to choose one shining coloured gate

It ended none of them were happy with their fate
They chose a partner of the opposite sex, a mate
and of the same nationality and colour
as learning another language was too much bother

continued

Africans chose the red gate as it was hot and bold
The Nordic people chose Blue as it looked icy cold
Europeans chose the Green as it was temperate
The Arabs never got a choice, they got the purple gate

Africans wanted to leave as there was poverty and war
Arabs wanted to move as there was no water to pour
Nordic's wanted sun and to wear big sunshine hats
Europeans wanted to get away from the Eurocrats

(There was not a Yellow gate as it was already full of Chinese.)

AFTERNOON TEA

My wife and I were invited to tea
We had never been there before
Detached house, nice garden, neat and tidy
Wife politely greets us at the door
They had children as we had
a sweet girl, very quiet, bright
The boy boisterous, noisy, normal
Parents were hard worker, money tight
Tea, sandwiches, cake, white tablecloth
Son said " Mum, she said "Quiet. More tea?"
Then offered cake,.,".Mum" " Quiet she scolded!
"You used my sheet as a Table-cloth." said he
The cake did not taste so good
unfortunately we already knew
That their son always wet his bed
Embarrassing for his parents, phew.

THE DANCING QUEEN

The dancing queen had a beautiful face
a fine example of the English race
With large brown, laughing eyes
Pink rose petal skin that cause men's sighs

Sparkling white teeth in straight line
set behind bow shaped lips, so divine
Natural brown hair, slick healthy, shining
arched eyebrows, forehead with no worry lining

On her nose was a silver ring
I suppose it's considered, the in-thing
I told her she was a lovely English rose
but the ring drew attention to her nose

Then felt impelled and had to mention
that it distracted men's rapt attention
from studying her excellent good looks
And then I got into her mother's bad books

Saying, you think it's an improvement, it's not
at a quick glance, it looks like dripping snot
A true event, I can get away with it as a rule
as I'm speaking from the heart, an old fool.

Note. I met this young lady called Jackie at Line Dance classes. She is a professional dancer. She laughed at my statement, but I thought her mother was going to explode.

STRESS Senryu

People get stressed
when illness causes trauma
Try to understand

BATU CAVE A TOURIST ATTRACTION

Malaysia, this country is a most interesting place
Batu Cave is huge and high up in a cliff face
Coaches packed with tourists eagerly arrive there
anxious to see the festival and enjoy the Indian fare
Colourful Indian foods set out on stalls and tables
spicy to entice thee, Pamphlets on the local fables

Ladies in Saris with long black tresses, selling cotton dresses
Men with hairless legs selling to people of foreign addresses
Steps up to the cave rise high up in the humid air
Those with disability and pensioners give up in despair
Flocks of pigeons patrol in packs, coo and plaster poo
intent on annoying and anointing those there to view

I climb, slipping sliding on slippery steps to view
holding the hand-rail peppered by pigeons too
I look over the hand-rail to find a safe track
there was a sinuous shiny snake, all black
A raging river at the bottom of the cliff base
full of detritus, detrimental to the human race

I did make it to the top, full of anxiety
The cave is huge, a great sight to see.
This river is a floating plastic trap. It should be
all collected there before floating out to sea.

Written in 2011.

BOMBS Haiku

Secular States
Peace-full integration required
Bombs explode every day.

ATTITUDE

It happened many years past
But a valid tale will last
It's about attitude and manner
Language, life, position and grammar
I was untidy, unkempt, in dirty working clothes
I'd been cleaning toilets, drains bins, all of those
I owned Alf's Café. This was a transport café
This is the story of a policeman's verbal gaffe

My occupation would be described as caterer
Rising at 4am to bake, I am the café baker
Mid-day, cleaning floors toilets bins, all of those
Drains are blocked; I require rods and a hose
I hurry down the old A31 in my old car
Police stopped me before I had gone very far
"What's the hurry 'Mush' where you running to?
"You're booked," and note-book flicked through

continued

"What for," I asked. He gasped "Speeding Mush,"
As he pushed me off the road into a bush
I replied, "I know why you picked on me
It was the gypsies that you were sent to see
They were at the transport café in Runfold
I'm an easier target, as I am alone and old,"
"Name and address and don't give me any tosh."
I quoted my name and address, which is very posh
His reaction was surprising, "Thank you Sir,"
I will look at the café to which you refer

Note. He closed his notepad, turned away and left
to attend the incident to which he was sent.
The term 'Mush' was a derogatory term

GREECE Senryu Year 2015

Thinking of the Debt
Greece might be a Russian Port
Grease my palm or else

MR DULL

He was quite tidy, big build and tall
like a six foot plain brick wall

No character in his face, it's like a ball
shows no emotion, no features that I recall

Like the moon, he hardly lights up the room
just a pleasant presence that lifts the gloom

continued

Conversation is limited to TV films or footy
Did speak of wanting a motorbike, a Malagutti

Did not ask questions, no information to share
Like the wall it is solid, it's there but it is bare

Any interests? I did not tend to ask
posing a question, seemed too much to ask

He smoked a large briar pipe with curved stem
nodded to speakers, as if he understood them

Puffing the pipe allowed him not to speak
which might have shown his intellect was weak

Note. A stranger in a coffee bar.

ARTIFICIAL INTELLIGENCE

I thought he was intelligent
But that thought soon went
The I-pod never left his clammy clutch
I realized that it was his mental crutch
Unfortunately, it makes him, out of touch
with people, by not communicating very much
While in a group his head was always down
eyes never met, he had a permanent frown
Oblivious to his surroundings, often on Skype
Lost in the Internet, in a dream-world of hype
Life is not in Facebook, Skype or Twitter
Acumen is not playing with a computer
Making your I-pod a mental crutch or tool
can end up making you look like a fool.

THE DIFFERENCE

I enjoy the sight of Sheiks and Bedouin
Touaregs wearing flowing coloured robes
I'm intrigued by the hair and hats of
Orthodox Jews with black clothes
The Rastafarian colours and decorates
his dreadlocks, demonstrating masculinity
Moslem faiths females favour veils and
Hijab's demonstrating faith and femininity

Sikhs are satisfied, showing their solidarity
by wearing smart silken turbans
All these faiths display their following
as do sporting teams and their fans
Christians tend to blend, difficult to define
Sometimes they proudly wear a small cross
The religious wear their clothes with pride
But a cross in the UK, can cause a job loss

COLOURFUL CATHEDRAL

Our road is a colourful Cathedral
With a constant cascade of leaves

Like fluttering moths, a sight to be seen
Creating a carpet for a King or Queen

When I return home and see such a display
I want to stay in the woods all day

The display is equal to any stained glass
The beauty of nature is hard to surpass

Year 2015

EYE OF THE BEHOLDER

She wears dingle dangle earrings
an ugly tattoo on each slender arm
A silver ring spoils her pretty nose
and wears plastic nails with stars
Assorted rings adorn the fingers
there are gold ones on her big toes
Wiggling, showing shapely legs and ankles
making her jewelry jiggle and jangle
When speaks, her tongue button glows

I think the human body unadorned
in its natural state and form is beautiful,
unless broken by bombs or blows
People are led and controlled by fashion
They wish to be different, but they are not
just following where the common herd goes
A tattoo can serve a useful purpose
A diabetic or could have one
on their fore-arm, where it shows

Or a warning message to doctors
saying, Do not resuscitate me.
so that your wishes, everyone knows
Surgery makes women look like dolls
hair, lipstick, lashes are enough to adorn
Character appears in facial lines, it shows
beauty is not in skin scarring, or metal rings
It is in personality mentality and deeds
it is not instant, it develops and slowly grows.

Note. A straight tree-trunk is boring. An old oak tree is very interesting as it is knurled and twisted. Surgery removes the character from an older face.

BEING GENEROUS

Generosity
is very often misconstrued
Better to be mean.

CATARACT

A hood over the head
oxygen pumped under.
My right eye is exposed

To occupy my mind
I pretend I'm in a tent with
light streaming through the hole

Liquid is squirted,
The eye is numb
but the brain races

A nice nurse holds my hand.
Her hand is small and warm
like my mother's tender touch

Snip-snip-snip-snip
like a leafcutter ant.
The lens is removed

Glaring light fills the space,
slowly a lens is slid in.
The warm hand has gone

continued

I ask, is it stitched or glued?
His reply surprises me,
pushed in like a bottle cork

Next day I remove the pad
to find I have wondrous vision
and colours not seen before.

B.G. 2016.

SATISFACTION

I am relieved
I feel an emptiness
I went to toilet.

A RHYME ABOUT LYME DISEASE

On a lovely hot summers day
when on the grass you love to lay
Bugs, and deer tick, a beastly thing
lay waiting for a warm body to cling

Some just want to bite and disappear
leaving large red bumps on your rear
But the Deer Tick unnoticed, walks around
until a succulent vein to suck from is found

continued

After applying an anesthetic; digs down in your skin
leaving its rear end sticking out; with its head within
If you do not notice it or have a sense of unease
after two days you might have contracted Lyme disease

Dartboard red rings emanate from the wound site
This shows you might have the disease, from the bite
Don't delay if a deer tick digs deep in you
for Lyme disease can paralyze you. It's true.

Note. It was in March that the bug bit me,
I was on powerful antibiotics for two weeks.

I wrote this as not many people realize how bad a bite from this tick can be and it is becoming more prevalent in the UK. I met a friend from the Parachute Regt that got bitten when on honeymoon in the USA and now cannot walk.

Note. Wherever deer are the ticks will be on the grass and on the bushes they will attach themselves to any warm-blooded creature.

MEN

Men go to war, why
They get guns, fed and clothed
Women pay the price

COCKNEY SLANG

Cockney rhyming slang is on
its last bacon and eggs
If you are not a Londoner
you'll be confused, its last legs
Londoners have been using it
for donkey's ears
which my interpreter says
means for many years

Do not assume that I am
a deep fat fryer
I have it on authority
that means a liar
And do not assume I'm
having a bubble bath
My dickie bird, that is word
is that it means having a laugh

Regarding bread and honey (money)
we lost our white Lady Godiva
which was the large white
five pound, paper fiver
Having expounded these thoughts
I'll don my weasel and stoat (Coat)
to buy a beer, a pigs ear
this rabbit has given me a sore throat

I will watch the custard and jelly
sitting in my Barrack Obamas
My teapot lids (kids) are amused
by my Stars and Stripes pyjamas.

I wrote this for and sent to American poet Aesthete2000.

MANKIND Senryu

Man has a problem
The trouble with humanity
there are too many

GROWING OLD

The trouble with growing old
are all the aches and pains
and no insurance when you travel
Quite often I have found that
pension plans that you have made
and long-term investments just unravel
We imagine that we are in charge
of our destiny, position in life
and always try to break the mould
We are just like sheep being driven
by forces we cannot comprehend
and unwittingly do as we are told
There is quite an element of luck
for I have lost many friends
on the journey to this fold
Calculated risk is better
than wrapping up in cotton wool
Then to children your stories unfold
People like to think of living forever
but there is no room for this
There is not enough room on earth
It is an obvious unwelcome truth
that you and I must die
to enable renewal in others birth

continued

If there is no development or change
everything stagnates, rusts and rots
even the stars eventually explode
Everything in the universe re-cycles
In a trillion years or so you might
reappear as a humble nematode
If you are still alive at fifty-five
don't be a couch potato
Before your spirit flies away
enjoy the scene, family and friends
Work at enjoying each moment
of every minute of every day
For some that died so young
I do not shed my tears
they enjoyed the sporting risks they took
Others have died; that took no risks
There is no balance sheet between good or bad
or everlasting credit for being good, in my book.

THE MONEY MAN

Poor Peggy said she had a proposal
but it was from a man of ninety three
She asked, why do only old men fancy me
When you left me in the hotel lounge
this ancient bore acting like a Toreador
offered to take me onto the ballroom floor

He told me of the world cruises he takes
and his house in the Cote d'Azur in France
Money made him think he had a chance
He said his wife of twenty-six years
was in a Nursing Home after a stroke
and he was lonely, what a nice bloke!

continued

He tried his luck with you dear wife
Cos he couldn't imagine we are married
Because I do not look bored and harried
I open doors for you, hold your coat
share drinks with you and morsels of food
These are the things that are misconstrued

SPRING

Time to forget those winter winds and icy cold
Spring means renewal and fresh colour to me
Watching for snowdrops to emerge, crocus unfold

As my lawns start to grow into velvet green
Daises poke up their heads as if to cheer
Elegant roe deer in two's, start to be seen

I see a seagull paddle his feet on the ground
imitating the sound of raindrops, then catching
worm's that rise up for fear of being drowned

Shaking the winters lethargy from our bones
I prune trees and see the fruit tree buds emerge
And we start to spring clean our homes

Then in the hope of hot summer sun
prepare for barbecues, and parties, looking
forward to inviting family, friends, everyone.

TELL WHITE LIES

Being generous truthful and honest
most often totally and badly backfires
Because people just cannot believe it
then accuse you of being thieves and liar's

I tried my best to be truthful and generous
It did not work. That's where the problem lies
No matter how much money or aid is given.
better to avoid the truth, if must, tell white lies

No matter how much food or help is given
because 'YOU CAN', by individuals, or Nation
Take care, it often it ends in accusations
of self-interest. Resulting in anger and indignation

Sadly, all my life I have seen, recipients
of charity with a wide smile. 'Wish you well'
but after receiving houses and State benefits
then wish for you to, 'Burn in Hell'.

Like the French revolutionaries did despise
all those with any sign of wealth
They were offered cake to eat, big mistake
many heads were cut off, that's bad for health

Twisted minds often think that all donors
are lucky 'B's that won the lottery of life
My experience is that most; have worked hard
and often suffered deprivation and strife.

KEEPING YOUR MAN OR WOMAN

A gold ring and a wedding do not make a marriage
nor grand reception and a pair of horses and carriage
You'll need determination, perseverance and courage
Neither is a bond created by material things
Life will throw many problems at you and it brings
both disasters and pleasures fit for kings
You have heard the saying, all work and no play
the next line might be, he or she will play away
Always ask your partner. What shall we do today?
It is not an easy path, mistakes not easily corrected
In times of stress, you'll feel beleaguered, tested
Be calm and settle arguments when you are rested

BE VERY SCARED

Humans will self-destruct in war
Sadly, it is in our nature
It's no use hoping for peace any more
Just look back at our history
Men and women will always fight
for rights, water, food and territory

When a country is dictated to by the army
and has rockets and nuclear weapons
controlled in the name of one party
Three minutes silence in six degrees below
No-one moves, talks or lifts their head
nobody dares to move, it's a choreographed show

continued

If you see everyone standing; so very still
when asked or ordered to do so
Reasoning says, there is no free will
Not one person has an adverse opinion
Because if they want to eat
they must be totally subservient, a minion

Everyone has reason to worry and be scared
Look at European history, and you'll find the
same reasons for suffering and millions dead.

Note. I saw on TV the North Koreans standing still
in rank and file in minus six degree chill.

SCHOOLING

The children of the Palestine Nation
require shelter, food and education

It is not the responsibility of the UN
and it's a possibility when they become men

If they cannot improve their life
the youth are likely to create more strife

And might want to punish their occupiers
with individual attacks bombs and fire

GREENBACKS AND BROWN PAPER

It is just a new name, Quantitative Easing
Printing money without the gold
It causes inflation, it is not pleasing
It's a fancy name, it's a game just the same,
In 1960 our house cost £2,200 pounds
Our lodger, a salesman called Rodger
purchased an E type jaguar to do his rounds
it cost the same as our house, crazy as it sounds
A case of the elite and you and me
Then a postage stamp or cup of tea
cost three old pence and
only one penny for a pee
There's a correlation, you will see
Now it's 2012 you will pay more
£180,000 for an average house
A top range car has this price; I'm sure
Many houses much higher I expect
Governments will keep Quantitative Easing here
Germans printed paper money in the war
like ticker tape, but that was small beer
Our children will have to get used to it
Youth have plenty to worry about and fear
Paying for third world Country bail-outs
and inflation makes our kids future unclear
caused by printing money, without assets.

Note. Greenbacks were renowned for being a safe currency, and the British pound was safe until PM. Brown sold all the gold.
Brown paper used to be called Bum paper (toilet paper).

SIEGE MENTALITY

If under a siege
You would tunnel for supplies
medicine and food

Senryu. Ref GAZA.

THE PETRIE DISH

The World is a Petrie dish
To us, full of food, sea of fish
Look at the astronauts view
to them it's small and blue

The dish fills with bacteria
they starve, get weaker, wearier
We have the same situation
it is a question of graduation

The bugs fight for food and space
It is the same for the human race
A world large, limitless, you wish
It is finite, has an edge, it's a dish

World of life forever, was Father's pledge
That's pie in the sky, we a small wedge
Small wedge of life, so called humanity
eating the pie, consuming the future, insanity

continued

Stonehenge people left us the stones
knowing they'd leave no trace but bones
Animals do not destroy their habitat
Humans create mess, worse than a rat

Grandfather spent a happy life in Surrey
Now everyone flies the world, why hurry?
Pass by the Airport, smell the aviation fuel
It destroys the ozone, there is no renewal

Human and animal alike, famine and war
Arms to fight for space, money, that's what for
To obtain food, water, space and light
for all creatures, great and small, it's a fight

On the hills, you can still enjoy the air
But industrial valleys choke in despair
Don't trust the politicians to put it right
they're omnivores that learnt to stand upright

We are all made from dust, stardust
and returning to that state is a must
Action must be taken, a new banner unfurled
or our children will witness, the end of the world.

Do you remember the Petrie dish? Used in biology lessons, the teacher showed a clean dish with a thin layer of purified gel. Then a smear of bacteria was introduced. It multiplied until it filled the dish and being unable to climb out, all the bacteria died having filled the space and run out of food.

WATER WARS CARBON TRAILS

A Supermarket has this sign
Every little helps
That sounds, just fine

Caring for the environment
Energy Efficient hand dryers
to help reduce our carbon footprint

But they buy and fly
blueberries from Argentina
Leaving carbon trails across the sky.

Only 2.5 per cent of World water is fresh
0.1 per cent is drinkable, at a guess
60 per cent of that fresh water lies
in ten countries that control supplies
Most of that fresh water is in Tibet
China rules there, the World will regret.
Africa and the Middle East
of water, they have the least.

Note. Desalination is too expensive for most Nations.
Countries that do not have sufficient fresh water or a sea must rely on keeping good relations with neighbouring countries.

EMIGRATION Senryu

People in poverty
due to global warming
Which way? North is best.

Desert sands are expanding

BILLY LIAR (Politician)

Billy liar, all he said was lies
He was clever but quite ill
He did not understand truth
his only interest was oil supplies

When his ship did founder
in shallow sandbank water
full of lethal jelly-fish
Declaring, "My voice is louder"

he climbed the vessels tall mast
and shouted from the crow's nest
"I will keep watch over you all
down there, while you last."

He unlike Blythe, his ship gone
his safety boat then did sink
Sharks then did eat all his crew
but he kept swimming on and on

He had no need for any haste
he had protection, so blithely swam
The sharks around him did not like
his toothy grin and bitter taste

To foreign lands he always flies
as he no longer has a ship
Wheeling dealing, talking hawking
his business deals he plies.

Can you guess who this is?

Note. Captain Blythe (Mutiny on the Bounty) saved his crewmen by sailing a small boat 6,500 km across the Pacific Ocean.

SAVE EARTH ARMY

I served two years Army National Service
It actually did me some good
Now, I think, all school leavers should

And be taught their world is being degraded
What we need is a Save Earth Army
Now you will call me really barmy

The young are sheltered from the truth
that the world is in a perilous filthy state
Only seeing holiday places that countries create

They need to see the polluted rivers
Shanty towns, harbours full of oil and mess
Industrial areas with people living under duress

Save Earth Army conscripts would
see the truth, build with resolve and courage
be set tasks to try and repair the damage

Create goodwill, instead of waging war
with soldiers and the supply of arms
Improve living standards with all those healthy arms.

Note. The oceans are producing more than half of the oxygen in the atmosphere and it absorbs the most carbon. Greenhouse gases are increasing acidity levels in the sea. Plastic pollution is killing many marine creatures and chemicals and oils are also killing or changing their body chemistry. If you want to eat fish you had all better be thinking about getting motivated.
Note. I was an advocate of joining the British Army. But I have changed my mind as our soldiers are taught to fight and when necessary kill but then they are persecuted as killers and receive no backing at all from their officers or government. 10/01/2016

A MOLEHILL Senryu

You make a mountain
Out of a tiny Molehill
There is no need to

ENERGETIC ALICE

She sits, no she perches on the high, office chair
Alert, like a cockatoo, head held high in the air

Tiny pink painted nails, flit around the keys
flitting feverishly like fire ant frenzies

Texting messages as quick as she can chat
Her speech is staccato, rapid fire, rat-a-tat

She can't sit still; she shimmies and shakes her bum
to the beat of the radio's drum, boom, da, da ,dum

Typing, text, invoices, letters, giving quotes
Scribbles on the pad, ear to phone taking notes

This rocket, an apt description, if held on the ground
would explode, remains conscious of all those around

Searching out orders, between high metal shelving
for bearings and bushes, then practices pole-dancing

Orders in, Parcel and Post, new stock on the rack
Prepare parcels for the Mail, check and pack

continued

A smile, an acknowledgement to delivery driver
A break. "Coffee boss." Offer of tea for the buyer.

She made me tired by just watching her for an hour
while she was working in my son's office.

LIFE INSURANCE

Too good to be true

Premiums increase yearly

Calculate the cost

LAWRENCE OF ARABIA

Lawrence of Arabia
tried to create the perfect Arab garden
He was their hero like Bin Laden
A man with a dream, soldier, dissident or
politician's scapegoat? How was he seen
Was he honest or regarded as unclean
Initially empowered with true belief
in a cause, hoping for lasting peace
Coercion by politics would never cease
Things have not changed over the years
Arab tribes couldn't agree then or now
They cannot agree, for oil is the sacred cow

FEAR Year 2014

Who is going to build a town every year?
It will be Britain's responsibility I fear.
This will be needed to accommodate
migrants coming through Italy's open gate
Economic migrants from all over Africa
that put to sea, are taken to Lampedusa

Then a train trip to wait in a Calais tent
This will cause distress anger and dissent
They wait to stow away in any way, to Britain
Housing is given there without work or strain
Who will pay the bill? The British taxpayer will
Politicians will feel it. The voters won't stay still

Ebola is the predicted world pandemic
African hospitals are closing to the sick
Ebola will speed across Africa and the Med
as people run from the sick dying and dead.

There will be more and more young emigrants
leaving the old, the dying and dependents.

Written 2015

AFRICAN ANGST

Africa suffers war and depredation
There will always be deprivation
A splendiferous continent being spoiled
There are too many people in this world

Those with strong will, will prevail
The weak will fall and die on the trail
Who pays for all those guns and RPG's
that children carry and kill with ease

Man is destructive he pollutes the air, the sea
He is a predator. Yes, that includes you and me
The Chinese can see the minerals, the potential
Their expansion in Africa will be exponential

IF WE CAN'T WHY CAN THEY?

Why is the UK so generous, so easily seduced
Family on holiday visa, she heavily pregnant
had their baby on the NHS within a month
while Schools and NHS funds, drastically reduced

Arrived destitute from South Africa, got a house
never ever worked or paid taxes here
No qualifications to tempt employment
Some pensioners here are poor as a mouse
My nephew waited on Council list for years
These visitors, within three months,
were ensconced in a Surrey Council house
It will all end in anger and many tears.

A FAULT

If you look for faults
you will find it every time
so take rough with smooth

TEARS AND FEARS

When people stand still in orderly rank and file
Bowing heads and crying out in dramatic style
All with carefully contorted face, but hardly a tear
All for the late Kim Jong-il. If not they'd disappear
When a country is dictated to by the army
and is controlled in the name of one party
Three minutes silence in six degrees below
Nobody dares to move, it's a choreographed show
When President John Kennedy died
Without outward show; I quietly cried
There was no need to show my grief
my quiet tears gave my anguish relief

This shows that there is something to fear.
in the country of North Korea.

PIRATES 2009

Pirates seem to control the sea
immigrate smugglers would agree
that Navies are unable to cope
that is plain for all of us to see

Pirates preyed on people and possessions
they were hung drawn and quartered
unless they had permission from
Kings or Queens piratical concessions

Let ships arm themselves to fight
these bandits of the oceans
as soon as a threat is perceived
Protecting the pirates is not right

Very soon they will feel invincible
are there nations they do not touch?
Next they will target cruise liners
passengers on them are vulnerable

Don't think ransoms are for bread and honey
You will be told of their poverty but that's
no good reason to attack our ships
guns will be bought with ransom money

2015.

MORE IS UNOBTAINABLE

More production more jobs, more immigration,
more consumption and more taxation
Scientists and Military want to conquer space
Why? It is a very expensive type of race
Politicians know immigration control is lax
they only want a growth economy, to tax
The world is too small for the expanding human race
Increasing temperature means new deserted space
the world will not remain gentle and temperate
People in deserts will move out or dehydrate
Others will drown in rising seas, low lying land
or die in tropical storms and mudslide sand
Countries are already drowning in water, I'm told
others so dry, water is worth more than gold
There are many signs that do indicate
friends will turn on each other in hate
You will fight when food and oil are short
already millions require help and support
The Chinese decreed with wisdom and foresight
One marriage one child, positive they are right
People protest about terminating pregnancy, abortion
The problem will be, food and water, how to apportion
the shrinking assets of food, water and living space
and energy in this shrinking, fighting, finite place
problems caused by man & woman's desire for growth
More wealth, children, space, you cannot have both
In times of plenty, and international trade
donations of money and food are made
Beware, in drought and when harvests fail
and natural and man-made disasters prevail

continued

When Russia has lost its harvest of grain
stopped exports, its own people to sustain
Prices will rise, shutters drawn, supplies cease
the poor will suffer, starve, catch disease
Borders will then be closed, walls then built
like North Korea, Israel, no feeling of guilt
There are families that have lived on aid for years
bearing children in the camps without fears
Countries will hold their stocks for themselves
quickly supermarkets will have empty shelves
Five million immigrants add to France's poor
Four hundred Tamils knock on Canada's door
The weather will increase the immigrants flight
fleeing their homelands when ethnic groups fight

Written August 2010

OUR WORLD

Earth can only support so much life
Man and woman are smothering
covering the productive land
This will bring starvation and strife
Palm Oil plantations in straight lines drive
across the small farms valleys and hills
that was once productive countryside
Now only rats and snakes will survive.
Palm oil is being invested in heavily.

THE OVERLOADED DINGHY

If you were in a rubber dinghy
full of young people, out at sea

And others in a similar plight
had sank and with painful plea

They cry “Help please save us all.”
as they all swam in the icy sea

But if you took just one child
you would all sink very quickly

So would you show you care
and then join them in eternity

Or would you practice self-preservation
and row away to re-join civilization?

Note. This needs careful thought as there is a strong in-built sense of self-preservation in all of us. This also makes me think that the UK is like a big dinghy

THE VICTIM Haiku

A beaten victim
Will always be a victim
Always downtrodden

BUMS AND TUMS

I really don't wish to be rude
why are there so many big bums
and wobbly tums? It's in the food.

"It is in my genes." They cry
and I think that they believe it
"I slim, then get fat again." They sigh.

Gastric bands are all the rage
Breast reduction, tummy tucks
The big girls are not yet on centre page.

Somewhere there is a chemical imbalance
or a damaging product in our food chain
that causes so many calls for the ambulance.

Artificial colours, hydrogenated fat, preservatives
flavouring, monosodium glutamate.
Everything wrapped in plastic, things like that.

Why is there little research? No slimming success
Why is nothing done to help stop growing fat
Because there is no money in selling less!

Some-where in mass produced food and drink
there are additives that affect our bodies.
Soon there will be a tax on body fat, I think.

Note. Joanna Blythman states in her book SWALLOW THIS. 12/02/2015. High fructose corn syrup has now been identified as the key driver of the obesity epidemic in the U.S.

HORSES AND WHIPS. USA Senryu

To keep immigrants out
Now barbed fences are built
Next there will be mines

ROLY POLY'S

Roly-poly pudding and pie
Bouncing bellies and bulging busts
How long before they die?

Carrying Cola as they crunch crisps
frequently resting due to breathing
Also aching backs and slipped discs

Why is it that now we see
people getting bigger, fatter
In my youth it never used to be

Perhaps because cows have been bred
to have bigger udders
for more milk, by being unnaturally fed

To increase the farmers yield
they feed chemical hormones
and cows are no longer in a field

Note. The feed contains hormones
which to increase their yield

GRAFFITI

When graffiti is all you see
It is not a place to live or be
For dull minds are living there
In a state of deep despair
Pen and paper or the internet
Is a much better bet
For a way to express feelings
to other human beings
They endlessly repeat their sign
calling out. This place is mine
Like a mating call of a toad
By this, other gangs they goad
Perhaps it is better to have tattoos
so to recognize other crews
They feel deprived, perhaps justifiably
Their message being, don't Dis me.

Note. 'Dis me.' Means do not dismiss me.

A PIE IN THE SKY

Earth is an island from a spacecraft's view
Too many babies, that's people. Take note
An island can only constantly feed a few

Politicians always pat the baby's head
If anti-abortion and anti-contraception
do not change their thinking, many will be dead

continued

There is a food shortage now, don't you know
People are starving right now, it will be worse
Nothing can continually expand and grow

Politicians have ships or super-yacht
They are havens in a crisis with crew
and stock of food and fuel, waiting for what?

Money can be made by short selling wheat
when the grain crops get ruined
Making profits when prices rise, that's neat

Wars and exploration of Mars cause me concern
let us settle for less, nothing grows forever
Why spend so much money on experiments like Cern

More growth, more jobs politician's cry, like a race
Do not join a race to ruin, Armageddon
Settle for less, less people, slow the pace

They pretend they can encourage growth
to get you all back to work, It's like
asking for speed record from a sloth

Easter Island population outgrew their isle
and ruined it by cutting all the trees
This, our island, our pie, ponder on it a while

The USA was nearly made bankrupt
by the Space and Moon landing programme, I pray
those you vote for, will not be stupid or corrupt.

HEY YOU

An example of modern English..
Tell me summink, tell me the truth
Do you think that I am a bit uncouth?

Don't ya like me latest dancing dress
or is it cos me air's in a bit of a mess

I've really got a lovely big firm bot
unfortunately it don't get touched a lot

I reckon my big breasts are the best
Ow about givin them a firmness test

Perhaps you think that ise still too thin
but you aint yet felt the warmth within

Perhaps you don't like the fag in me gob
but I don't do drugs, I'm not a nob

I wanna be me, just the real me
and have you always next to me

When you taste me cooking, you'll feel a king
then at scrawny women you'll stop looking

Ere let me get me mitts on you, don't struggle
let me show you how I can lurve and cuddle

When you've touched me pale porcelain skin
and felt the deep desire that I have within

I will make you salivate with a dream
of my peach pie with cherry and cream.

KABUL 2021

Airport Destroyed!
International crisis
USA gives AID?

WHY THE RED HEAD?

You can see him a mile away
He is a flaming redhead that's why
He's like a poppy in a cornfield
Seen in a blink of an eye

The red apple shines at you. Eat me!
to birds that fly up high in the sky
For propagation, red fruit seeds
then fly far, that's the reason why

Red poisonous frogs warn, I'm dangerous
His blood, his genes are what we need
say the female frogs, for our protection
Like the poppy, red helps spread his seed

Neolithic women wanted redhead men
Like the bee exchanges pollen for nectar
And the men were not all that shy
for red fruit seeds will always travel far.

SHORT ON WORDS Year 2009

Ear, ere....Wot's ere
An ear....Wot ere?

Yes....Who's ear!
No fear....Its is ear!

In your mitt....oose is it?
A lofty toff....I bit it!

Ee tackled me. Twit...So Is ear I bit!
Now it's in me and....Grand, aint it

Dedicated to Robert Acraman. Para Regt.

A FIGHT Senryu

You may start a fight
If I feel vindicated
I will finish it

COLOURFUL LEAVES

Poetry words are like colourful leaves
drifting across spaces in your mind
Then like certain leaves that catch your eye
when written down in poem or prose
disappear from short term memory
as quickly as those Autumn leaves
whisk away in the winter winds

THE COLD MORNING

As I drive the lonely road and study
the trees and plants in winter hues
It seems to echo my thoughts and views

I meander along this misty track
Remembering my last evening of delight
when you were in my arms, my sight

In the coldness of early morning
Full of inner turmoil and yearning
was so distracted, I missed my turning

Across the road was a fallen oak
Pulled down by an entwined ivy band
around its trunk, now too old to stand

How pretty the ivy looks, like you
Young and slender, wrapped around the tree
which felled the once proud oak, like me

It stopped me in my stride, my track
laid across the public right of way
I had to turn around and go away

With you the obstacle is not so clear
You say “My love is not there, till I die
but your lips, your touch does this belie.

Note. This was in written in 1979 when Peggy said she did not wish to see me any more. I wrote her ten poems and she relented.
We have been married for 41 wonderful years.

OBESITY

I see more Easter egg shapes each day
It makes me sad, I have to say
When I see fat children, I feel despair
that the parents, do not seem to care
Children following parents, in procession pass
with a walk, waddling along like a ducks arse
obese children walking with a rocking motion
Nobody dare comment to avoid confrontation
A cursory look at their shopping basket
reveals why they will soon occupy a casket
Food that makes cooking redundant, easier
Bread, pies, Cola fizzy drinks and pizza
We all want our children to have long life
avoid illness and the Surgeon's knife

Sugar is a culprit, it affects the inner body
Triglycerides are altered, bad for everybody
Palm oil in pastry, chips and crisps is to blame
It tastes so nice and it's cheap. That is a shame
It is in 10% of products in the supermarket,
So returning to mums home cooking is my target

Notes. Check out, American Heart Association on triglyceride's.
National Institute of Diabetic Digestive and Kidney Diseases on palm oil.

I was nine and a half stone at the age of 21 and got to 15 stone working in my café, I ended up having open-heart surgery and the recovery from that was the most painful experience of my entire life.

OFFSHORE COMPANIES

Pandora Papers
See what politicians do
And get away with

Senryu

WIFE AND LIFE

Life is never perfect
as there always be strife
Mine is perfect right now, due to my wife

In all walks of life and business
there will always be Ups and Downs
People can't be perfect, you'll always meet clowns

We have lost money due to dodgy people
But I am content and don't have any regrets
as at the moment, we do not have any debts

I believe there is a creator of the universe
and feel Christian but never go to church
I'm Zen Buddhist; don't leave people in the lurch

I was so lucky to have been born in England
in between the 1st and 2nd World Wars
Sad to see wars started with so little cause

We are so fortunate to live in this blessed country
Britain; quite small, protected by the gulf stream
such a pleasant environment, so fertile so green.

POLITICAL WORLD

We are so very lucky
to have a wonderful world
Destroyed by governments

Senryu

BEING TIDY

You've been untidy all our married life
and very difficult to live with
said my very tidy, lovely wife
(She might read this)

You do not put your clothes away
I said I will wear them again
for another time or day

I cannot be all that bad though
I won a medal as the smartest soldier
Royal Engineers at Farnborough

She calls me 'Wooden-Head'
which is rather unkind
I keep quiet, in order to get fed

I am not such a careless dunce
I save you washing them
if I wear them more

THE WADDLE

They walked with a waddle
their cheeks wiggle and wobble
Chewing and chomping in unison
Fat mum, fat daughter, fat son
holding potato crisps and cola in their hands
they will all soon be requiring gastric bands

MY PLEASURE

A warm hand gently caressing
The suns warmth, a blessing
To feel the wind ruffling my hair
Rain in moderation, then fair

A warm safe place to sleep at night
To gaze at nature with gift of sight
A drink of cool fresh sparkling waters
To bear healthy sons and daughters

To be able to watch their growth
and hope they do not suffer sloth
Avoiding famine, pestilence and war
I wish such a lot, but nothing more

THE BARRISTER

A chameleon can change its colours
as I see it, so can she
Educated, elegant poised and pleasant
not hoity-toity, mixes well with others

The eyes, soft brown, doe- like
walks with swift fluid motion
Hah, but wait, so does a snake
glide, until it rises for a strike

Warm, but when in hushed courtroom
that warmth turns to icy blast
like an arctic wind on your face
with an intent to create, an air of doom

Looking soft, like butter on a summer day
she cuts to the bone
as a butcher cuts a carcass
and lays the joints out on a tray

Feline like a cat with impassive face
that when on an attack
show the incisors of a killer
used with precision, for the Coupe de Grace.

Note. I watched her perform in the courtroom.
It made me cry out involuntarily.
So I got escorted out of the courtroom

FREEZING SNOW

Freezing snow outlines branches of the trees
Especially the broad branches of the oak
White expanses expose the field's boundaries
On the Hogs Back, seen from this height
Man-made hills, quarries and lakes
are exposed in stark black and white
Houses, like Chess pieces on chequered board
never noticed before, hidden in the Surrey Hills
Of this versant view, I never get bored
Everything in contrast, black and white
Tracks of foxes, dogs and dainty deer
to the inquisitive eye a pleasant sight.

AFRICAN BLOOD DIAMONDS

Ivor rode in a fine white carriage
but his horse had a smelly behind
He sought buried treasures
his lover had bid him to find
Lover don't find another, she wrote
I promise you my body and troth
I now have a child out of wedlock
Will you pledge to care for us both
He traded in Blood diamonds, then
paid girls to escort him, rather sad
They called him sexy tornado
he ended up with Aids and quite mad

Note. There will always be trading in Blood Diamonds.
This was written for a poetry competition.

DREAMS

Dreams of Ivory towers and clean blue sea
Shiny new cars, Mall's with indoor snow to ski
150mph big cars which are just for show
With speed cameras there is nowhere to go

Gin palace yachts full of model's, ship ahoy
Sail away to avoid the common herd, the Hoy polloi
Lots of yachts don't go to sea, just sit and rust
in the salty yacht basins of the upper crust

Man is destructive, he pollutes the air, the sea
He is a predator. Yes, that includes you and me
The Chinese can see the minerals, the potential
their expansion in Africa will be exponential

Unfortunatley now for the likes of you and me
The world is a such a dangerous place to be
Unless you're in a government position with
police and army protection or sailing the sea.

OUR WET WORLD

As the polar ice completes its thaw
We are told that twenty kilometres of land
will be under the sea, then a there will be
a hundred million people displaced or more

continued

The world was once clean, now I despair
What I see around me is now in decline
water shortages, bad air quality, rising sea
It's not renewable; it is in a state of disrepair

A perpetual time machine, you all might
think, it is not as the dish will quickly fill.
All space will be filled and Countries will fight
for all land within their reach dig and drill

Note. Even the Arctic, deepest depths of the sea and even the Moon.

A CHRISTMAS TOAST

I do not need a decorated Christmas tree
Winter frosts provide everything for me

This turns teardrops of morning dew
into lights hanging on tips of yew

They twinkle in the bright morning sun
at no cost, they are free to see by everyone

Together with the shiny red berries on the holly
backed by dead leaves golden glow, don't be sorry

They not only give you a festive view
it's a warning that winter is now due

Robins search for grubs, raking leaves over
Roe deer dig, eating my lawn moss and clover

Winter time, for renewal, a cleansing time
Let us toast to Christmas with a glass of wine.

BELIEF

If you can feel the suns heat
from an object so, so far away

If you have seen a child grow
from your seed to be an adult

If you can have thought
which you can turn to speech

If you understand that stars explode
to create clouds of gas and dust

And can understand that you
are created from that Stellar dust

If you can dream of something
then it is possible for it to happen

Then you will understand
Why there is belief in a creator

WINTER Senryu

North wind is blowing
I think when it is snowing
Time to hibernate

MULTIPLE SCLEROSIS Bernie Green, written on behalf of my eldest son

I am fighting the battle against M.S
That's short for Multiple Sclerosis
Slowly, inexorably creeping like wet mud
MS takes my energy, leaving me dud
I see the pain in a loved one's eyes
I stood tall, now I can only lie and sigh
First a cotton wool foot I felt, and then a fall
I wish now that I could manage a crawl
The creeping numbness started in my toes
Slowly, upwards, until everything goes
While others sleep, I often don't get a wink
I wish I could reach and pick up that drink
In the night I cannot even reach a bell
Nor can I take a deep breath to yell
Sometimes in sleep, I dream how I used to run
Rode horses, motorbikes, before MS begun
The nights are long, lonely and full of fears
I think of what was and is; I cry some tears
There is longevity in the family tree
Why did MS choose to pick on me?
Don't dwell on life's balance sheet of what is lost
The credits are, life and family; but death the cost

BEING OLD Senryu

A fresh coat of paint

why? The house is warm and dry
and soon I shall die!

A QUESTION

I had a small yacht in the 1960s
Which I kept at Chichester Harbour
The Harbour holds millions of tons of water
which flows in and out with the tide
A flow of seawater at about seven knots
Why has this power has never been utilized
I believe that this alternating force of water
can be used by an under-water turbine

BEAM ME UP

Don't put me in a box with golden handles
when my due time is up
Do not shut or lock me up
for I am phobic, claustrophobic
This is my wish, my burning desire
please send me up in smoke, in fire

You can't make lamps out of me
for I don't have any tattoos
for you to scalp and amuse
Do not preserve this soft watery parcel
in aspic, plastic, formaldehyde or ice
when old and dead, it's not very nice

I'd like to think, away from man's stink
that I will be free to float around.
I'm sure that parallel universes abound
And I hope it's not dark and dank
when my creator decides my time is up
like Star Trek Scottie I will say "Beam me up"

continued

My Mother did, her spirit flew away
so peacefully. I have this silly dream
like her, I'd like to ride up a sunbeam
The Doctor dashed, but I said, "It's OK"
Do you know I never cried
for my Mum, the day she died

The sunbeam was shining on her head
I'm in the hospital by her side
I felt her go on that sunny ride
Things you make, build, create
are quickly lost, broken, gone
but memories are very long

Like a vapour in each other's mind
You, me, we, to be or not to be
a person is not what you see
You can visualize, all past times good and bad
Where letters, photos can disappear in strife
memories will stay with you and beyond your life

In my mind are those times with Mum
when conversing over a cup of tea
telling secrets only known to her and me
I've had much excitement, dives and dashes
so spread my dust in the garden bower
Perhaps, I can come back as a fragrant flower.

DEATH

I am not going to 'Pass away'
or 'Sleep the long sleep' I'll be dead
Nor 'Resting in peace.' I'll be dust.
I don't want my remains lying around
an empty case just getting in the way.

I won't be having a "Long sleep in Eden
or joining angels to play the harp
I will be dead deceased, departed
cremated, gone and forgotten my
ashes spread in our gorgeous garden

I do not want to go more-rotten and stink.
Hopefully my chemicals will be re-used in the
growth of a beautiful flower or a butterfly.
Can you imagine me as such a delightful thing?
Far from how many people view me now, I think.

IN PASSING

His eyes opened, could not cry out
Pain gripping his chest like a vice
He died peacefully in his sleep.

Note. I have tried to write a Senryu or perhaps it is an epicedium. Last line his epigraph. A heart attack can be bloody painful.

AUTUMN

The Autumn leaves adorn the trees
with colours to suit a King or Queen
Gold and yellow and shades in between
We aged humans tend to be more sedate
wearing drab colours, a rather dull display
of browns and blues, greens and grey

As the trees die in a blaze of colour in
a final show of absolute ostentation
A friend of mine dies in another nation
Aesthete2000; sadly a poet I never met
and yet I felt her warmth from so far away
This loss has left me feeling in total disarray.

Note. This lady helped me with my poetry and persuaded me to write, which has been a most interesting and rewarding experience for which I will be forever grateful to her.

Sadly, she has passed away but she is on my mind nearly every day.

DUST TO DUST

When you and I are turned to dust
This unfortunately becomes a must
with no brain in what is left of you and I

A million trillion years will pass easily by
Enjoy this journey; slow is better than direct
the destination might not be what you expect

THE LAST ACT, ON ME

My last act will be
to fertilize the garden
You may then pee on me.

Senryu

COP 26

CLMATE CHANGE IT'S AFFECT AND SOLUTIONS

People are starving in this world and it is not something new. Aid agencies have been feeding various nations for years, this created sitiuations where people were becoming dependent on aid.

Others started to emigrate to countries that they think can provide facilities for a better life.

Politicians are not talking about the fact that there are too many people in this finite world.

In some countries women are having as many as six children whereas I believe in the UK two is the norm. Women should make the decision as to how many children they bear.

Women should also make the decision as to abortion as they are the ones that bear the brunt.

continued

More people, more houses, more roofs more roads equals more flooding, and less land for agriculture.
More houses more roads means more concrete which has a global warming affect.

There are many poems in this book about this subject and I am quite happy for the use or publication of these if you give due credit to me which is an Intext citation to me.

BOOKS BY BERNARD. A. N. GREEN

DUNCE OR DYSLEXIC by Simpleton. 401 pages. 40 photos. Bernard Green was co-founder of The British Parachute Association which is now named British Skydiving Ltd. Autobiography.
ISBN 978-0-9576042-0-9 Published 13/November/ 2015.

MY WIFE AND CANCER Non -fiction.
A true story, not about treatment or medicine, but about the problems faced by a couple when their partner suffers cancer. 192 pages. 2 photos. It is not a sad story.
ISBN 978-0-9576042-5-4 Published 27/November/ 2015.

BUILDING THE KHUFU PYRAMID Non-fiction.
Shedding new light
How did the Egyptians lift forty-five ton blocks of stone nearly to the top of the pyramid? The author has a solution. This has been approved by Professor Menno of the faculty of Mathematics and Natural Sciences of Groningen, the Netherlands.
Paperback 31 pages 6 photographs.
ISBN 978-0-9576042-4-7 Published 01/October/2015.

PARACHUTES, POEMS & POLEMICS Autobiography. Poetry and Prose.
This book covers early parachuting in the UK.
My first jump was on the 9th July 1958. A free-fall from 1,500ft. This was not sky-diving but just falling and it was dangerous. Adult reading. 312 pages. 22 photos.
ISBN 978-0-9576042-1-6 Published 04/March/2016.

RURAL LIFE IN RUNFOLD DURING WORLD WAR TWO
Autobiography. Bernard's life as a child during WW2.
His adventures and the times with his father on Black Market deals. He skipped school and spent his time with the soldiers that were billeted in the huge local houses. 100 pages of surprizes, things that health and safety would stop these days.
ISBN 978-0-9576042-6-1 Published 16/July/2018.

ZEPPELIN L15 & THE WAKEFIELD GOLD MEDAL
Narrative non-fiction, educational.
It tells the story of Sir Charles Wakefield. Lord Mayor of London 1915-1916 and the 353 beautiful 1oz gold medals that he produced for the RGA gunners that shot down the first Zeppelin over London.
170 pages. 88 illustrations.
ISBN 978-0-9576042-2-3 Published 12/September/2018.

ADDENDUM TO THE BOOK
ZEPPELIN L15 & THE WAKEFIELD GOLD MEDAL
This book lists 264 named individual medals out of the 353 Gold medals that were issued and interesting family stories.
ISBN 978-0-9576042-8-5 Published 15/December/2020

SPIES IN VUNG-TAU 1915-1920
SAILING THE G.L. WATSON 'RAINBOW' Photos of Vietnam.
Nonfiction, Historical. A true story that came about from Victorian glass photographs that had been lost for over 100years. It took 2yrs to research. It records where the French placed Naval guns in the mountains of Vung-Tau in case the British invaded.
198 pages, 111 Greyscale photos & 7 colour.
ISBN 978-0-9576042-9-2

BRITISH SKYDIVING IN THE 1950's
Autobiography. The Author started the very first Skydiving School in the UK after training with the French Military Skydiving School at Chalon- Sur-Soane, France.
The author was also the co-founder of the BRITISH PARACHUTE ASSOCIATION and the first secretary. His company name was BRITISH SKYDIVING LTD and had three clubs at the aerodromes Thruxton , Wiltshire, Halfpenny Green near Birmingham and Stapleford Tawney in Essex.
The Association are now using the name British Skydiving Ltd
198 pages, 51 Illustrations.
ISBN 978-1-913218-84-3 Published 01/January/2020

DEGRADATION OF THE BLACK PEOPLE

Narrative. Non-fiction. The attitude towards Black People began to change in the 1st World War when American Soldiers arrived in and around London to help defend Gt Britain. Then the British realized that they were fighting in Europe.
In the 2nd World War they had their own fighter aircraft squadron called THE TUSKEGEE AIRMEN.
129 pages. 128 photos and illustrations, 113 coloured.
True stories. Old Comics, Trade Cards, Greetings and Post-cards.
Readership-Secondary and Adult.
ISBN 978-0-9576042-7-8 Published 08/March/2022

www.ingramcontent.com/pod-product-compliance
Ingram Content Group UK Ltd.
Pitfield, Milton Keynes, MK11 3LW, UK
UKHW061952290726
14090UKWH00021B/1193